Our Future Selves

Our
Future Selves

NESTA ROBERTS

FOREWORD BY
LORD AMULREE

London
GEORGE ALLEN AND UNWIN LTD
RUSKIN HOUSE MUSEUM STREET

FIRST PUBLISHED IN 1970

© George Allen & Unwin Ltd 1970

SBN 04 362017 5

PRINTED IN GREAT BRITAIN
in 11 on 12pt Juliana
BY CLARKE DOBLE AND BRENDON LTD
PLYMOUTH

ACKNOWLEDGMENT

All works of contemporary history are a group enterprise, though convention dictates that only the name
of the author appears on the cover. This one is the
co-operative product both of the many individuals
concerned with work for old people whom I have
consulted while writing it and of the far greater
number who, over the years, have helped to give me
some understanding of the subject.

Above all, its final form owes an incalculable
amount to the encyclopaedic knowledge, the precision
and clarity over complex detail and the inexhaustible
patience of the Secretary of the NOPWC, Miss M.
Bucke.

The National Old People's Welfare Council
acknowledges with gratitude financial help from the
Company of Armourers, Sir William Butlin, A. S.
Cohen Trust, Goldsmiths' Company and Lever Fund
which has made the writing of this book possible.
The Council is also grateful to Lord Amulree for his
interest in providing the Foreword.

The National Old People's Welfare Council was set up in 1940, while the country was engaged in war, with Eleanor Rathbone as its chairman: a remarkable example of foresight and humanity among a people who it might have been thought were otherwise engaged. Since that time it has carried out a fine and useful work in establishing branches, and there are now about 1,500 of these, in the counties, county and municipal boroughs. On these local committees sit representatives of all organizations, both voluntary and official, who have interest in the welfare of the aged. While there is much that can be done, and in many cases more that should be done, by official bodies in providing, by statutory means, accommodation of all sorts – hospital, home, hostel and special housing – as well as some of the other amenities of life, there is an enormous amount of work to be done in securing the wider welfare of these people that can better be carried out by voluntary agencies. The local Old People's Welfare Committees do a great work in ensuring that the right support is given to those who need it: this is carried out in an imaginative and flexible way which would be difficult under the necessarily more rigid procedure of official bodies.

Miss Nesta Roberts has now given a detailed account of how this Council was first formed, what was the background to its formation and what important work it has done for the betterment of the aged since its foundation. The increasing number of elderly persons in the country makes it all the more important that there should be some organization responsible for their welfare and to assist in trying to solve some of the many problems that appear to afflict the elderly. There are many questions, too, that are posed by the aged which need intelligent and sympathetic answers. This the National Old People's Welfare Council, under its two active chairmen – Miss Rathbone and Mr John Moss – has been able to carry out with conspicuous success: there is no reason to suppose that this record will not be maintained by the present chairman, Mrs Newman.

This book is a useful record of what has been done since 1940: both Parliament and the voluntary organizations have done a great deal to improve the lot of the elderly, and particularly of those elderly who are destitute of either money or friends. This is all set out in Miss Roberts's book and the story should be of interest to the many people who care for these matters and, at the same time, should give a lead to those whose sympathy has been aroused but who are uncertain how best to turn this to a practical use.

The late Sir Stanley Unwin was interested from the start in the making of this book and his help and assistance in making possible the publication of the work is greatly appreciated: it is sad that he should have died before he could have held the finished volume in his hands.

AMULREE, M.D., F.R.C.P., Consulting Physician University College Hospital, President, British Geriatric Society

CONTENTS

CHAPTER I

Old Age

'Altogether there was great diversity – of people warm-hearted or reserved; illiterate or well-read; enthusiastic, garrulous, witty or disconsolate; sociable or isolated from nearly all human contact. Some things people had in common. They were, for instance, rarely self-pitying. They bore pain with surprisingly little fuss. They were anxious to appear honest and fair-dealing, liked a joke, were easily pleased, disliked formality or affectation, and were rarely content unless they were of use to others and had company. This was written into their manner, their conversation, and their homes. They thought of themselves first as members of families and work-groups, as grandmothers, aunts, or housewives, as grandfathers, uncles, and cabinet-makers, and only second as individuals old in years.'

Peter Townsend: *The Family Life of Old People.*

Old age, like death and road accidents, is something that happens to other people. We call road accidents a problem, implying that something can be done about them. We do not speak of death as a problem, because there is no solution for the inevitable. Curiously, since it, too, is inevitable, old age today is more and more often referred to as a problem. Old age, it is worth reminding ourselves, is no more a problem than childhood is a problem; it is a natural state. Many old people have problems. Some are peculiar, or at least special to their age group. Some are common to us all, but bear more heavily on certain of the old because they may be weaker, or lonelier, or poorer than the rest of us. But the 'problem of old age' is in fact the problem of youth and middle age. How can a proportionately smaller number of people of working age support and ensure the well-being of a proportionately larger number of people of pensionable age, which, at the time of writing, is sixty for women, sixty-five for men? (Though happily, at any given time, large numbers of these two age groups would not be considered 'old' since they would be healthy and active, some, indeed, still at work, for statistical purposes pensionable age remains the most practicable definition of the elderly.)

Long term estimates based on population projections are notoriously inaccurate. The unforeseeable factors can vary from the losses of young men in World War I, through the wave of migrations set off by the Irish Potato Famine, to the recent invention of the contraceptive pill.

Even mid-term forecasts tend to be imprecise. In 1942, for example, the Beveridge Report prophesied that, by 1971, the elderly would make up more than 20 per cent of the total population. Ten years later the Registrar General, in his Return for the fourth quarter of 1967, estimated that the pensionable (sixty-five-plus) population of England and Wales would probably be 16·4 per cent of the total population in 1976, 16·3 per cent in 1981, 15·2 per cent in 1991 and 13·5 per cent in 2001. In round figures that means that whereas, rather more than fifty years ago, one in fifteen of the total population of Britain was elderly, ten years on the proportion will be almost one in seven. There is a tendency in some quarters to say rather glibly that the reason is the progress of modern medicine, notably the discovery of antibiotics which 'keep old people alive'. Certainly they are a contributory factor; but the main one is that there are many more old people to keep alive, partly because the birth rate in the early years of the present century was a high one, passing even the post-war peak of 1947, and partly because of the remarkable decrease in infant and child mortality. In 1900–2, when the average annual death rate was 148·7 per thousand of the population, twenty-two of those deaths were of boys under fourteen, and nineteen those of girls under fourteen. In 1950–2, with an average annual death rate of 103·2 per 1,000, the corresponding figures were 3·2 and 2·5, decreases respectively of 85 and 87 per cent. Put another way, the expectation of life of a boy born in 1901 was forty-six years, that of a girl fifty years. For a boy and girl born in 1951, the expectation of life is respectively sixty-six years and seventy-one years. With it all, there has been no appreciable lengthening of our life span. 'A ripe old age' remains much what it has always been. The difference is that more of us live to reach it, and that, today, men and women in late middle age are perhaps more active than they were 100 years ago, though prodigious exceptions to that generalization will immediately come to mind.

What is, perhaps, peculiar to our own day, with its mania

for categorizing and pigeon-holing, is our tendency, in our concern for the old, to think of them as a race apart. From the beginning of the Christian era, to go back no further, there is evidence that they were cared for, if only because the Beatitude 'Blessed are the merciful', with its corollary 'for they shall obtain mercy' needed an object for its fulfilment. This is not to suggest that compassion has, in any age, been an exclusively Christian quality. In our own, in fact, the Jewish community provides for its elderly in a fashion which is an example to all.

The church in Jerusalem was so busy with good works that the apostles appointed deacons to look after the 'daily ministrations', so relieving themselves of the burden of 'serving tables', but there is no mention of the old as such among those to whom they ministered. No doubt some of them were old, as must have been some of the 'widows in their affliction', and the sick, and the 'poor of this world rich in faith' with whom St James was preoccupied about the same time, but they are not singled out for that reason. Stepping over 1,500 years, even the most specific petitions of the Litany do not mention the old. They are taken in with 'all that are in danger and necessity and tribulation', or 'all that are desolate and oppressed'. That is not to say that no attention was paid to the special nature of their needs. N. W. Faxon's *The Hospital in Contemporary Life* (Harvard, 1949), which Professor Townsend quotes in his survey of homes for the aged in this country, tells us that, by the third and fourth centuries AD, the Eastern Church had got so far on the road to special care that it had separate institutions for the aged, for the sick and for the infirm poor. It was to be the better part of 1,600 years before we rediscovered such civilized and enlightened ideas.

Whatever might have been the standard of care in those early institutions, at least, it would not have been patronizing. These were Christ's poor, whose service was at once a sacred charge and a means of working out one's salvation, whether by directly caring for them or by providing the means which made such care possible. Also, no blame or shame was attached to poverty as such. There is a fascinating minor field of study in the development of the idea that poverty is of itself disgraceful. To some extent, probably, it is related to the growth of man's capacity to control his environment. When natural

15

disasters – which, at that time, included the ravages of the invader – were frequent and defences against them largely ineffective, poverty could be seen to be a visitation rather than a vice.

In a more sophisticated society, in which the forceful and prudent could rise, be it on the backs of their brothers, they would naturally tend to feel that those who sank had only themselves to blame. Later, ameliorating circumstances were recognized, as comes out very clearly in Victorian novels. The godly middle classes could become impoverished when banks failed, the 'respectable' working classes when the breadwinner was carried off by a fever, both common enough hazards of the time. The ungodly, clearly, owed their misery to profligacy or gin, according to their station in life, and could expect no sympathy and little help. Today, in Britain at least, the wheel has come full circle and the most wretched are seen, not as culpable, but as the helpless victims of their own personal inadequacy. (The reverse spin is due any time now; not any longer 'Pull yourself together!' but 'Have you taken your Largactil?'.)

Meanwhile there are still places in Ireland where nobody has yet learned to call a beggar anything harsher than 'A poor man', or 'a travelling man'.

In Britain beggars inspired the beginnings of statutory social services. For centuries they were virtually non-existent. A closely structured feudal system, whatever its iniquities, meant that there was a place for everybody and everybody was expected to keep it. The monasteries looked after the sick, the destitute and the incapable, as, indeed, they continued to do, with greater or less efficiency, up to the Dissolution. The change came with the beginnings of an industrial society which, like the great churches of East Anglia, was built on the backs of the sheep. Once the man who could find no work at home had at least the prospect of finding work in the woollen manufacture of a neighbouring town, a mobile society, (and so, ultimately, however long it was deferred, an incoherent society) was inevitable.

At worst the situation produced by the roving bands of the able-bodied who had failed to find work was akin to that of immediate post-war Europe, when Displaced Persons lived as best they could. 'Hark! Hark! The dogs do bark! The beggars are coming to town!' was no nursery jingle in those days. It was a warning to householders to lock their doors and make sure the poultry was in the yard. 'Sturdy beggars' were harshly punished; the old and the crippled or otherwise disabled were licensed to beg their bread. A sequence of interim measures culminated in the landmark of 1601, the Poor Relief Act, which made every parish responsible for its own poor. At this stage the programme was not haphazard. The able-bodied were to work, the children were to be bound apprentice, or at any rate to be placed in employment. The incapable, defined specifically as 'the lame, impotent, old, blind and other persons who were unable to work' were to be relieved. In each parish the churchwardens, supported by up to four of the more solid citizens, were appointed Overseers of the poor, with responsibility for raising, in cash and in kind, the means to put these measures into effect. For many, probably the majority of the incapable, relief meant admission to the new Poor Houses which were set up under the Act. At a time when the old monastery infirmaries had ceased to exist and the voluntary hospitals for the most part had not yet come into being, they were almost the only resort for the helpless, the hopeless, the mentally sick, the very young and the very old. The miscellaneous asylum which resulted was to persist virtually unchanged up to the time of the Poor Law Commission of 1832–4, and, with modifications, into our own day. It is necessary to say 'almost' the only resort, for private charity, besides establishing annual doles of bread, blankets and the like for pious widows of the parish (the 'deserving poor') also, here and there, set up alms houses where the aged might live. It is worth noting that the formula of independence and privacy within a group, with, usually, some degree of surveillance, and without separation from the local community, has never been bettered and is being repeated in today's flats or grouped bungalows with a warden on call. Even the compulsory prayers which we would regard as an imposition would not be likely to have caused any great resentment at a time when church-going was still a custom.

How well the system obviously thought out with care really worked in practice we shall never know, since the aged and helpless who were among its beneficiaries have left no testimony. At least it held the situation for more than two centuries. During that time the Poor Relief Act (1722) gave the parishes power to set up workhouses to supplement the few Houses of Correction which had been established independently, where, in intention at least, the able-bodied poor were to be given work which was useful, not merely punitive or time-filling. Later, under the so-called 'Gilbert's Act' of 1783, came institutes specifically for the sick and aged, which were built by groups of parishes which had banded together for the purpose.

As the Black Death and the collapse of the feudal system had brought the Elizabethan Poor Law into being, so the enclosures and the unemployment which followed the Napoleonic Wars led to a public inquiry into its functioning. (Poor Law Inquiry Commission, appointed 1832.) By that time the system had degenerated to an extent that would have made it unrecognizable by those who had framed the Act of 1601. Little or no work, purposeful or otherwise, was accomplished in the institutions which sheltered an unclassified horde of inmates which included most categories, from the moribund to the layabout, from the infant to the senile. Outdoor relief was given to the able-bodied in cash or kind (sometimes both) without any obligation to work for it. Allowances, sometimes regulated according to the number of children in the family, on the lines of the family allowances paid today in many European countries, included the disastrous Speenhamland system operated in Berkshire, where the justices decided to make up the wages of all workers to a certain subsistence level. This, at a time when there was no minimum rate, was, of course, a guaranteed method of ensuring that there never would be one.

Unrest reached its peak in 1830, when a 'labourers' revolt' in South-east England was followed by a savage 200 death-sentences (all but ten of them were commuted to transportation). The country was shocked; the Government had already been concerned about the cost of relief. Heroic reform was the brief for the Poor Law Commission, which sat from 1832–4. They concentrated on dealing with the abuse of the Poor Law, particularly by the able-bodied who drew out-relief, and the remedy they suggested was based on the notorious 'less eligibility' principle. Relief, that is, was conditional upon living in the workhouse, and the workhouse must be seen to be so much more undesirable than the sufficiently bleak world outside that nobody in his senses would wish to enter it. (In fact, a fair number of those who did find their way there were out of their minds.) There was no particular intention on the part of the members of the Commission to subject the old to a punitive régime. There was, indeed, some intention that the new workhouses or 'unions' should be of different types, so that the residents might be classified. It was not carried out and the aged, save for the lucky few who found a place in an almshouse, or, much more rarely, in one of the voluntary hospitals (Guy's Hospital was established in the eighteenth century to treat the aged sick for whom St Thomas's could find no room) were bundled with the rest into what a later report was to call 'a human warehouse'. The deterrent effect of the policy was undeniably successful. There was bred into successive generations of the old a fear and horror of 'the house', and of anything connected with the Poor Law, whose last traces, persisting even today, colour the attitudes of a few of the most intransigent of the aged towards anything connected with the Ministry of Social Security.

CHAPTER II

Origins of Welfare
for the Aged

'. . . there exists, we regret to say, no inconsiderable class of old men and women whose persistent addiction to drink makes it necessary to refuse them any but institutional provision. For this class, indeed, the Aged Poor of Bad Conduct, out of all the pauper host, it might well be urged that the Destitution Authority at present makes a not unsatisfactory provision. For old men and women of this kind, the General Mixed Work-house, with its stigma of pauperism, its dull routine, its exaction of such work as its inmates can perform, and its deterrent regulations seems a fitting place in which to end a misspent life.'

It can have been given to few members of public bodies to convey so much information in so little space as did the four signatories – Beatrice Webb was one of them – of the Minority Report of the Royal Commission on the Poor Laws of 1909. In 100 or so words they reveal the essentials about the social conditions and the social climate of the day, about the general mixed workhouse and about its eventual patrons. There is no reason to doubt that there was indeed 'no inconsiderable class' of aged men and women who drank too much. Drink, 'the quickest way out of Manchester' as it has been called, must have been for many of them not only the quickest, but often the only way of escape from the intolerable circumstances of their lives. The gin palace waxed against a background of deplorable housing and an almost total absence of opportunities for recreation. It waned, with due respect for the efforts of the Temperance reformers, as the conditions of daily life improved. In the generations of which the members of the Minority Group were writing, it was inevitable that there should have been a fair proportion of misspent lives.

Nor, given the temper of the time, was the critical attitude of even the more progressive members to be wondered at; it was shared by all but the most exceptional social reformers in a period when poverty tended to be seen as evidence of moral failure rather than as the inevitable consequence of certain economic phenomena. It should be noted, too, that the appointment of the Royal Commission in 1905 was itself a token of a desire to separate the relief of the distressed from the condition of pauperdom which had been gathering strength over the past twenty years, the Poor Law Board having meantime been succeeded by the Local Government Board. Harshly as its members may seem to us to have expressed themselves, they came out unanimously for liberal measures including the replacement of the general mixed workhouse by classified institutions and the provision of old age pensions and State insurance against sickness and unemployment. The Minority Report even wanted the Ministry of Labour to be established 'to organize the National labour market so as to prevent or minimise unemployment'.

Of how little had been done to carry out the classification recommended by the original Commissioners of 1834 we have ample evidence. Florence Nightingale, campaigning for the appointment of trained nurses to workhouse infirmaries, has left searing accounts of what conditions were like for their patients. Mrs Margaret Neville Hill, founder of the Hill Homes for old people, has childhood memories of the Cambridge Workhouse towards the end of the last century, when 'the old inhabitants were almost prisoners, for they were seldom allowed out, and had to wear a curious, heavy, unattractive clothing which marked them out in public. They were expected to do what work they were capable of in return for a little extra tea. They had virtually no personal possessions and nowhere to keep anything. I remember going to the workhouse one summer's day and finding about twelve babies' chairs in the little courtyard. Into each chair a baby was put in the morning, sitting on a little pot. Their aged nurses fed them but did not move them all day and when they were tired they laid their heads on their trays and slept. The baby-sitters had no option about the charge laid upon them.'

An Inspector's report on the same workhouse in 1911 shows that Miss Nightingale's reform still had far to go. 'The nursing

21

staff,' he wrote, 'was wholly inadequate. It consisted of one partially-trained nurse who was responsible for the whole of the nursing and also for the maternity work, with a woman who came in from the town to sit at night. It was quite evident that a great deal of the nursing was done by the paupers. The majority of the bedridden were helpless and the wardswoman whom I observed feeding the women was not a proper person for this duty. There were few nursing appliances and no modern conveniences. There was not a slop-sink in the whole infirmary and the female side was destitute of any water supply except for a drinking-water tap fixed over the basin in such a way that no vessel larger than a mug could be placed under it. There was no provision for a sink or for hot or cold water.'

At about the same time, the late Dorothy Keeling, later to become the founder secretary of the Liverpool Personal Service Society, and, later still, first secretary of the National Old People's Welfare Committee, was then, as an eighteen-year-old school leaver, taking her first steps in social work under the auspices of the Brabazon Society, at Bradford. Her responsibility was to teach netting to chronic sick and bedridden men in the Bradford Workhouse. Of this initiation into what was to be her life's vocation she wrote: 'The dreary lives of these men and their unattractive surroundings made a great impression on me, so that I always returned home from my weekly visit to them worn out, physically and mentally, and fit for nothing except to lie on the sofa for the rest of the day.' More than sixty years later she still spoke with horror of the hopeless vacancy to which these old men – for most of them were old – were condemned. This, at worst, was the régime which the destitute and helpless aged could expect. At the time when the Royal Commission reported there were 140,000 of them in Poor Law Institutions, and the Minority Report drew attention to the fact that no more than a couple of thousand at most were in classified establishments.

Where these existed, to the credit of an uncommonly progressive local authority or an inspired individual, since the central policy was alike for all, the 'deserving' old did indeed enjoy better quarters, better food – the Commissioners noted 'a cheap and wholesome currant cake to their tea' at one establishment – more liberty to come and go. Kingston-upon-Hull had even gone so far as to buy up terraced houses and convert them into cottage homes for old people. An enlightened Master or Matron could do a good deal to make life more tolerable for them (just as, conversely, today, rigid and unsympathetic staff can make the most lavishly appointed home alien to old people). The bulk, who made up almost half the workhouse population, spent their last years in an environment which drew from the Commissioners such comments as 'defective in every particle'.

Old Age Pensions became a reality in 1908, while the Commissioners who had recommended them were still sitting. The weekly five shillings, even though it was subject to a means test, and not paid until the pensioner had reached the age of seventy, was a godsend to those outside institutions, whether they lived alone or with a family which could support them only with difficulty. Those in institutions, and the workhouses, as provision for other categories of need improved, were more and more associated with the old, were at the end of the queue in what was an era of remarkable social reforms. The 1914–8 war would, in any case, have checked progress. In theory, the transfer of the powers of the Boards of Guardians to Public Assistance Committees, which came with the Local Government Act of 1929, should have hastened it. But immediately ahead were the years of the Depression, when local authorities were apt to be more concerned with finding ways of saving money than in branching out in new expenditure, which major reforms would have entailed. Advances there were, however, with, more surprisingly to those who believe that respect for the rights of individuals and a generally permissive attitude are strictly contemporary growths, evidence of a new outlook here and there.

The report of a conference on Public Assistance organized in 1937 by the County Councils' Association and the Association of Municipal Corporations is a rich source of information, both on current achievements and on current ideas, beginning with the declaration of the chairman, Lord Courtown, that 'the deserving poor, who fall to be assisted by the Public Assistance service, are no longer considered, because of their destitution or poverty, as only a shade better than the wastrel'. Sir Kingsley Wood, then Minister of Health, who followed, urged the importance of providing 'new types of accommodation to meet the changing needs of our time'. He was concerned about the infirm old, for whom there should be 'some more homely type of accommodation than the general workhouse can supply'. Such accommodation should have 'small dormitories, and even single rooms, small day rooms with ready access to the garden and cheerful, homely surroundings, without . . . any of the atmosphere of the workhouse'.

From official intention to local practice is often a fair step. In that year, 1937, there were still hundreds of children living in workhouses, in flat contradiction of the Public Assistance order, so we should not be too surprised that, even today, in our purpose-built small homes for old people, the principle of single rooms for all is not universally followed. At the same meeting, Mr John Moss, later chairman of the National Old People's Welfare Council, then Public Assistance Officer for the County of Kent, presented a paper which offered a country-wide panorama of the various experiments which were then in being. He began with a reminder that, almost forty years earlier, the Local Government Board had recommended that the privileges accorded to inmates of institutions who were sixty-five years of age and over should include 'sleeping accommodation in separate cubicles' and went on to outline the kind of provision for the old which was made in certain European countries, notably Scandinavia. We have cause to blush still at the comparison between even our new, small homes and those of Norway and Sweden thirty years ago, when it was taken for granted that people would bring at least some of their furniture and personal possessions with them when they entered a home. But, scattered as they were, England had its growth points.

Bradford, in its thirty-year-old Daisy Hill homes, had fifty-six bungalows consisting of one room and a scullery, where residents prepared all their meals except dinner. Dartford, Kent, had converted two private houses into homes respectively for forty-five aged men and forty aged women. They had a 'good supply of easy chairs' and the old people had 'absolute freedom' to wander around the grounds and go in and out of the home as they desired. They were, it was confidently reported, 'very happy'. Manchester City Council had taken over three houses as homes for old people. There was a bowling green and the residents had 'a great deal of liberty'. They could go out daily and have visitors every afternoon. The LCC had converted three Victorian houses at Clapham into a home for 100 men. The dormitories varied in size from three beds upwards and each man had a chair, a locker and a bedside table. There were small tables in the dining-rooms 'as are now provided in many institutions instead of the old-fashioned long, narrow tables and forms'. Paid staff were employed for all domestic work. Both the matron and the assistant matron were nurses. It appeared to be 'very desirable' that there should be a nurse on the staff of any such homes because of the possibility of collapse among aged people. Southend Public Assistance Committee had provided for the use of the aged at the Rochford Institution 'a bowling green on a piece of land which was formerly used for growing cabbages'. At Quinton Hall and Highbury, the Birmingham Board of Guardians had homes for old people where, although they were large – 160 and 200 beds respectively – there was 'absolute freedom' for the residents. They could go out daily until 7 p.m., or later with permission. They were not allowed to wear their own clothes but they did have their own caps or hats and 'each man has a locker where he can keep his personal possessions and his Sunday suit'. Bristol City Council had decided to accommodate 288 aged and infirm men and women in six houses, each for forty-eight residents, in which, besides central heating, the sitting-rooms had open fire places. Denbighshire County Council, at Wrexham, had provided for old people 280 beds in 'a large and airy pavilion' which the Ministry of Health had described as 'in many ways a model for similar institutions in other areas'.

Northumberland County Council was aiming at securing the amenities of a household for its old people by accommodating them in homes with twelve beds, which could be divided into two sub-units. For the bedridden there would be infirmary units, each with two wards of six beds and two single wards. Christchurch, Bournemouth, through the generosity of a private donor, had adapted a portion of its institution as 'a superior type of accommodation' for 'the more respectable type of aged woman', and the whole institution was 'noteworthy for its pleasure gardens and garden plots which have replaced the potato and cabbage plots normally found in any PA institution'.

Interesting as these details are in themselves, they are even more so for the light they cast incidentally on the general situation. The institutions described were sufficiently remarkable to be singled out for attention against a norm in which people slept in large dormitories, sat on hard chairs, looked out on cabbage patches diversified by concrete, were separated according to sex and, except on one day a week, could not pass the gates without permission.

At this time, besides old people in PA institutions, there were about 8,000 or 9,000 who lived in voluntary homes, large or small, religious or secular. The Salvation Army, the Church Army and the Methodists, among other religious groups, had been pioneers in establishing small homes that aimed at creating an atmosphere of domesticity even when they could not be luxurious. Roman Catholic religious orders usually ran large, infirmary type homes which nursed their patients to the end. Other small homes were established for retired members of various trades or professions. A homely atmosphere is more easily created in a small community than a large one, and small numbers, in theory at least, should make formal rules less necessary, but it would be wrong to assume that the fact that a home was run by a religious organization or a voluntary society of itself ensured the happiness and well-being of the residents. Many of them tended to be spartan in their equipment, certainly by present day standards. This was seldom the result of a deliberately penitential policy in homes run by charitable or religious organizations, even if some of them did impose a way of life which would not have been adopted voluntarily by those who did not share their faith or philosophy. Thirty years ago life for most people was a good deal less materially pleasant than it is today. The middle classes, for example, accepted icy bedrooms as a matter of course. Also, when funds had come from contributors whose donations were the fruit of their own self-denial, there was naturally a feeling that every penny should be made to go as far as possible.

In any case, those in residential care could scarcely have lived more frugally than the old outside, eking out an existence on the Old Age Pension and what savings they had, with or without Public Assistance. Preoccupied as we very properly are today with what remains to be done for the old, we sometimes forget how the conditions of their lives have been improved, even if it is only as a result of a minor share in generally higher living standards. Social workers whose experience goes back to the thirties often remember details which one overlooks, as, for example, the great advance in cheap ready to wear clothes, and the relative ease with which modern fabrics can be washed. Today we are questioning the principle of concessions for the old, thinking it better to ensure for them an adequate income. Before the war they had neither. There were no wireless sets for Old Age Pensioners, the television did not exist, practically speaking, there were no Meals on Wheels, there was no chiropody service, there were no reduced fares on trams or buses, there was absolutely no margin for entertainment in the weekly budget. When, in 1928, the Liverpool Personal Service Society set up a committee specifically for the care of the elderly its workers found two old ladies, aged respectively seventy-nine and seventy-eight, who lived at Garston and who had never ventured as far from home as the Liverpool landing stage.

It would, of course, be a mistake to suppose that no voluntary work for old people had gone on before the founding of the Liverpool committee, which was the first of its kind in the country. Victorian literature is studded with references to visiting the old and bedridden, with comforts which included beeftea and Bible-reading (the word 'comforts' is not used ironically here – it was a period when many of the old were both devout and little more than semi-literate). Nearer our own day there were cinema proprietors who offered free or reduced price seats to Old Age Pensioners on certain afternoons. The general scope of social work inevitably included some help for the old. The distinguishing feature of the Liverpool committee, of which Miss Eleanor Rathbone was the first vice-chairman, was that it existed solely to further the welfare of the old. Miss Keeling recalls that, by 1938, it was running monthly social afternoons for the elderly at twelve centres, serving between them about 1,000 people. Miss Rathbone, typically, had suggested that the aim of those who volunteered for such work should be to take the place in the old people's lives of the sons and daughters whom they had never had or with whom they had lost touch. So, between the monthly meetings, the helpers tried to keep in personal contact with as many as possible of the old people, helping them both personally and practically. They extended their services to those in the local institutions, finding that, in Belmont Road Institution alone, there were 240 people who never had a visitor and 'never received a letter, a flower, a card or a book'. The committee made good those lacks, organizing a library service, and, in 1929, supplying pillow-phones to 200 bedridden old people. So, empirically, needs being met as they arose or were discovered, was laid the foundation on which has grown our present complex of services for the aged.

Liberal ideas found support among statutory officers also, even if they were not widely spread. At the Public Assistance conference mentioned earlier, Mr Moss pleaded the importance of placing old people in institutions near their previous homes, of allowing them to bring some of their possessions with them when they were admitted, and to wear their own clothes, of giving them pocket money, and of accommodating the bedridden in small wards where more attention was paid to comfort than to hospital spit and polish. Above all, 'the general comfort of the occupants should be the first consideration', said Mr Moss. 'They should be able to spend their declining years in a quiet atmosphere of kindly homeliness, free from the restrictions which are necessarily found in large, general institutions. Every assistance should be given to old people to enable them to live in their own homes. Housing authorities can do much by providing bungalow dwellings, and possibly even one-room dwellings, for Old Age Pensioners who are capable of looking after themselves.'

Many local authorities, as Mr Moss went on to say, were already providing houses of this kind, and the Ministry of Health, in its most recent report, had said that 'arrangements made under the Housing Acts can provide for the majority of the aged people who are able to look after themselves'. The report added, however, 'there is no sign that the demand for accommodation under the Poor Law is decreasing'.

Contemporary readers are likely to be struck by the fact that, while Mr Moss and members of the conference who took part in the discussion mentioned the need to find staff who had the welfare of the old at heart, and would create a homely, warm atmosphere, nobody hinted at any difficulty in finding staff at all, which is one of our gravest current problems. What would have grown from this scattered but vital leaven if the work had developed naturally? We can only guess. Two years and a half after the Public Assistance conference we were at war. Old People got no special consideration in World War I. Before World War II was well under way, a national committee had been established to watch over their welfare.

ADDITIONAL SOURCES USED FOR CHAPTER II

Margaret Neville Hill: *An Approach to Old Age and Its Problems.* Oliver & Boyd (1960).

Dorothy C. Keeling: *The Crowded Stairs.* The National Council of Social Service (1961).

Public Assistance Conference, 1937: Final Report Published by the County Councils Association and The Association of Municipal Corporations.

CHAPTER III

The Founding
of the NOPWC in 1940

Wars create some problems, others they simply reveal. The best-known example of the latter is the evacuation of children from the slum areas of our great cities on the outbreak of World War II, which revealed to a horrified Britain how the submerged tenth lived. For old people the two processes were intermingled. The upheaval of the war had done much to make their lives more difficult even before the bombing raids started in 1940. In that year, which saw the pensionable age for women lowered from sixty-five to sixty, the Government decreed that old age pensioners who needed additional help should, in future, receive it not in the form of Poor Relief, but as a supplementary pension, granted by what had formerly been the Unemployment Assistance Board and was now simply the Assistance Board. Two things happened. As always after a progressive measure affecting the nature or availability of some benefit – and this applies equally in other fields, such as medical treatment – more people applied for it. There were many who, rather than have recourse to the hated Poor Relief, had struggled on in bitter poverty. When the responsibility was passed to the Board, they were able to overcome their pride. Within a few months the original 275,000 assisted pensioners were augmented by another 750,000. (It may be noted here that, by 1946, the total number receiving supplementary pensions had risen to one and a half millions. Near the end of that year the basic pension was increased to a more realistic figure and the number of assisted pensioners dropped to about half a million.) Second, officers of the Board who visited old people in their homes to ascertain their needs saw how acute those needs were. They realized also that many of them could not be met simply by an increased allowance.

The sequel was typical of the climate of English social work, in which, at its best, despite periodic waves of mutual mistrust, and misunderstanding, both voluntary and statutory agencies accept that they have something to give to and something to learn from each other. In this instance the initiative came from the statutory side, the Board, or certain of its representatives, thinking that the National Council of Social Service might be able to help. Two years earlier the NCSS had in fact convened a meeting of representatives of statutory and voluntary bodies to discuss the kinds of social service which would be most necessary if and when war, then clearly threatening, was declared. There resulted the concept of the Citizens' Advice Bureaux, the first 200 of which came into operation on September 4, 1939, the day after the outbreak of war. Eighteen of them were in the Liverpool area, and, five months later, Dorothy Keeling, who had been deeply involved in the case work from which they had been born, was seconded to the NCSS to develop the service nationally. As head of the CAB department of the NCSS she and Miss D. Ibberson of the Assistance Board, acting as a private individual, were among a small group of interested people who met to consider the problems of the elderly and what might be done to help them. Together they drew up a list of bodies who might be concerned and should be invited to attend a conference on the subject. It is worth reproducing in full, if only for the evidence it provides of the amount and variety of social work from which, potentially at least, the old might have benefited, which was then going on. Represented at the conference, which took place at 26 Bedford Square, the headquarters of the NCSS, on October 7, 1940, with Eleanor Rathbone, M.P., in the chair, were the Charity Organizations' Society, the National Women Citizens Association, Rotary International, the London Council of Social Service, the Church Army, the Institute of Hospital Almoners, NALGO, the Salvation Army, the Friends of the Poor, the Women Public Health Officers' Association and the Assistance Board.

Invitations had been sent also to the British Association of Residential Settlements, the Churches' Group, the Freedom Association, the Goldsmiths' Benevolent Institute, the Ministry of Health, the National Union of Townswomen's Guilds, the National Conference of Friendly Societies, the Queen's Institute of District Nursing, the Royal Masonic Benevolent Association, the Scottish Corporation and the Co-operative Women's Guilds. In those confused days, the fact that they did not reply was as likely to have meant that their headquarters had moved or been bombed out of London as that they were uninterested or felt unable to help. Eleanor Rathbone spoke for many when she said that in spite of the 'peculiar difficulties of the times', which later generations or other nations may consider to be an engaging understatement, she believed that a National Committee which could survey the provision for the aged and take responsibility for their general welfare was badly needed.

The situation as it was portrayed at the conference supported her view. Out of 25,000 old people in London who had applied for assistance, 17,000 were living alone. Many were living on top storeys, and ground floor accommodation, when it was offered, was often entirely unsuitable. Relatives living nearby, with whose help the elderly had just been able to manage in such adverse conditions, had often been called up or moved out of London. Those who could afford domestic help could seldom find it, since the former domestics had mostly found themselves more attractive and more lucrative jobs. Many of the elderly did not know that they were entitled to the services of a District Nurse if they were ill and it was said that some doctors did not call upon District Nurses to visit their elderly patients as often as they might have done. Many of the elderly did not know either that, if they were receiving supplementary pensions, they could be placed on the permanent medical list of the PA authority without having to make a separate application to the relieving officer each time.

For those for whom residential care was desirable if not essential, the prospect was equally bleak. Few local authorities had acted on the official advice to set up small homes for old people; in the majority of areas accommodation for them was still in the old mixed institution. There were too few voluntary homes and there was no general register and no system of inspection of those that did exist. All this, and a good deal else, was brought up at the conference, which ended with the passing of a resolution that the societies represented should be invited to serve on a committee whose task would be to co-ordinate, or try to co-ordinate, the work already being done for the old and to extend its scope. The new committee would have power to add to its numbers; the NCSS would act as convener. The Committee for the Welfare of the Aged, as it was at first called, had come into being.

It met for the first time during the following month, having appointed Eleanor Rathbone as its chairman, and, at the outset, proved the need for its existence. The Ministry of Health, it was reported, was anxious to evacuate from London 'old men and women over sixty-five, in normal health, who should be away from the strain of incessant bombing'. The British Red Cross Society, the St John Ambulance Association, the NCSS and the WVS had been asked to help with the task of finding accommodation for them. Local branches of the NCSS were making inquiries about available empty houses where numbers of old people could be quartered, also about households able and willing to offer a home to one or two.

Emergency or not, the first idea was riddled with pitfalls, and the committee laid them before the Minister in detail. It was not advisable to leave old people in houses to look after themselves. They would need help with the heavier work and a certain amount of care and supervision. Above all, they should not be left without a responsible person in the house at night, a condition which applied equally to houses which were run with the help of a part-time organizer.

The committee pointed out that, though the scheme was intended for old people in normal health, it should be borne in mind that even the normal elderly usually needed a certain amount of personal care and assistance, and billets should be arranged only in households where this could be provided. Also, the upset of moving, combined with the coming of winter, was likely to make them fall ill, and specific arrangements would be needed to provide them with medical and nursing care. The expense of this should not fall on the households concerned.

It was clear that evacuation was the overriding problem of the elderly at that time, and the committee agreed that, for the present, it should devote its attention primarily to the hardships arising from it. They were varied, and some of them, it seems to us with hindsight, were so obviously foreseeable that only the conditions of the time could excuse the absence of any official effort to provide against them. Institutional problems, as members of the committee commented, were a peacetime as well

C   33

as a wartime question, but immediately there were grounds for believing that many old people who had been evacuated from their own homes in danger areas were miserable in their new surroundings. It would, indeed, have been astonishing only if they were not. The committee decided to investigate their treatment by first finding out from the LCC where the old people evacuated from London had, variously, been sent, then asking local organizations to visit them and report to the committee. At this stage, of course, 'local organizations' did not mean branches of the NOPWC, which did not exist; the available agents ranged from the Women's Institute to the Vicar. Additionally, the Minister was to be asked whether he was considering the appointment of social workers to look after the welfare of old people evacuated. For their part the members decided to find out what was being done for the bedridden and infirm who had remained in danger areas. Apart from the difficulty of getting them to public shelters, it was pointed out that many liked to stay in their usual surroundings, and the possibility of reinforcing the basements of the houses in which they were living so that they could be used as shelters should be suggested to the authorities concerned.

At this first meeting the new committee began to exercise its right to increase its membership, both by representatives of additional societies and by individuals who had much to contribute in their own right. One of the latter, Mrs Margaret Neville Hill, Chairman of the Hornsey Housing Trust, was a pioneer in the provision of homes for the mentally frail among the elderly. Another, Miss Olive Matthews, was an essentially English type of free-lance social worker, or perhaps 'social agitator' is a more precise description, who did much to draw public attention to the housing needs of old people. More will be heard of both later in this book.

Two months later the problems of evacuation were still at the head of the list, and the difference of attitude, perhaps, rather than opinion, between official and voluntary agencies was becoming increasingly clear, with its consequent underlining of the need for a body like the Old People's Welfare Committee, the name which was adopted in January, 1941. Dorothy Keeling had a discussion on institutional problems with the Ministry of Health, which said that the institutions to which

5,000–6,000 elderly Londoners had been evacuated in the autumn of 1940 were now emergency hospitals, and so were better equipped and innocent of the old Poor Law stigma. The first was undoubtedly true. Whether the old people who entered them realized the transformation which a change of administrative status had wrought in buildings whose outward semblance remained identical seems at least questionable. However, the Ministry's representative had agreed to put the committee in touch with its Regional Officers in Manchester, Leeds, Birmingham and Newcastle, who could say where the elderly evacuees were and whether visiting might be desirable.

On its own account the committee, which, from the start, had been concerned about voluntary homes, had obtained lists of those run by the Church Army, the Salvation Army and Roman Catholic orders, and intended to seek information about others by means ranging from an approach to the Public Trustee to inquiries from churches.

Having been reminded by a hospital almoner that when OAPs had been in LCC chronic sick hospitals for thirteen weeks, the LCC was no longer able to draw a pension for them, and so ceased to allow pocket money, it asked Miss Irene Ward, M.P., to press in Parliament for the issue of a circular, reminding local authorities of their powers to pay pocket money out of the rates. The Mental Health Emergency Commitee felt there was need for arrangements other than removal to large institutions both for those senile people who should be evacuated and for those who were now left alone all day because relatives who had previously cared for them had to go out to work, and the committee agreed that it should be co-opted on any special sub-committee which might later be appointed to consider the welfare of the senile aged. Records of successive meetings show the fight for pocket money going on and more and more schemes for visiting in emergency hospitals being arranged locally. The organizations involved Councils of Social Service, Guilds of Help, Mothers Unions and the WVS, besides clergy and ministers and interested individuals. In some areas visiting schemes had been set up before the committee's prompting and there were interesting examples of local enterprise. At Bury the CSS had found private billets for some of the single evacuees and had set up a hostel for married couples. The Liverpool Personal Service

Committee had made a grant from its funds to provide comforts and pocket money. A list of guiding principles for visits to institutions was approved by the committee and copies were sent to both the organizations undertaking the visiting and to the Medical Superintendents concerned. In the rare instances where there was opposition to visiting schemes the committee's prompting became firmer and more insistent. By May, 1941, visits had been arranged in forty emergency hospitals, thirty through the NCSS and ten independently. Easington Board of Guardians were reported to be 'not in favour of strangers visiting'.

The Vicar was asked to approach the hospital authorities, with the proviso that if he got no satisfaction the matter was to be taken up with the Deputy MOH for Durham County.

This proved not to be necessary since, by guile or by grace, the Vicar was able to overcome the objections of the Guardians.

Inquiries about voluntary homes were being pursued and letters asking for information about them which were published in the *Nursing Mirror*, the *Universe*, the *Church Times*, the *Christian World* and the *Guardian* brought in as a bonus many offers from private householders who were willing to provide accommodation for individual old people, usually at about £3 3s per week. Private billets were needed: a recent meeting of the Ministry of Health Committee on the Evacuation of the Aged had reported that 900 were waiting to leave London, of whom 400 were considered suitable for private billets and 500 for hostels. Most pertinently, Roger Wilson of the Friends' War Relief Committee, pressed the point that billeting was not a haphazard procedure. The personal help of social workers was needed both in choosing those to be billeted and in choosing the billets to which they should go.

There was no progress with the problems of the infirm old; the Minister had 'regretfully' decided that no beds could be provided for their evacuation to safer areas. Miss Rathbone and Miss Keeling, a gently inflexible couple, waited upon the Ministry and the outcome was an agreement that the Ministry should press on as quickly as possible with hostels on the outskirts of London to take the old who had been bombed out of their homes, and that these hostels would receive the infirm also. The matter was the more urgent because relatives or others responsible for them were often themselves prevented from seeking shelter during air raids.

By now money was becoming a problem. It was clear that the work would expand rapidly and expenses with it. The sums mentioned read quaintly today. Three hundred pounds, it was said, would enable the work of the committee to be carried on for a year. There was talk of trying an appeal to the USA, source of hope in so many spheres at that time, but finally it was decided that members should write privately to friends on the other side explaining the aims of the work and its needs. The next mention of fund raising was at the July meeting, when it was announced that the BBC had offered the committee time to make a broadcast appeal.

Lloyd George was the first favourite on the committee's list of those who might be asked to launch it. If he was not available, members suggested Edith Evans, Eleanor Rathbone herself, Flora Robson, Sybil Thorndike, Marie Tempest, Rose Macaulay or Rebecca West. It was a glamorous group, even if it is difficult to find the common factor in all its members, for certainly they were not all over sixty. In the event, Lloyd George being unable to oblige, Eleanor Rathbone suggested more soberly that Dr Maude Royden be asked to make the appeal. She consented, and the total amounted to more than £2,000. This was wealth; not only did it ensure solvency for the next two years, it made possible the setting up of a loan fund to enable organizations and individuals to establish homes for old people of limited means who were too infirm to live alone but who were not hospital cases. The provision was to be extended to those who had not been bombed out. Again one is struck by the modesty of the sums involved. Loans envisaged were of amounts up to £200, to guarantee rent for the first six or twelve months. Applications from local committees for small grants of up to £5 for postage, travelling and so on, would be considered. By this time twenty-nine replies had been received from the societies which had been asked to set up Old People's Welfare Committees. Four already had them; eighteen were considering setting them up. The seven refusals did not necessarily imply that no work for the elderly was going on in the areas concerned, but more probably that established organizations saw no need to set up a new body. It was stated also that the maximum needed to run self-supporting homes was 32s 6d per week per resident, and that if the Assistance Board would recognize generally the principle of making up what old people could pay to the sum needed to make approved homes self-supporting, it would both help in their establishment and enable loans to be repaid in a reasonable time. In this the NAB proved co-operative. It undertook, 'in certain circumstances' to increase supplementary pensions for aged applicants for homes to make their total income 30s per week.

By now the committee had prepared a draft list of homes charging £2 weekly or less and was busy getting out a list of more expensive ones. Since it was obviously not possible at such a time to press the Ministry of Health to inspect new homes, local OPW Committees were asked to inform the central body of any in their areas which were unsatisfactory. For its own part, it set up a Homes Sub-Committee and considered the advisability of forming a federation of organizations in charge of homes for old people. Relative affluence encouraged also effort in the direction of propaganda, information and what might be called missionary activities. A leaflet making clear that supplementary pensioners could be placed on the permanent list of the PAC was circulated to Citizens Advice Bureaux and sold on bookstalls for a small sum. A leaflet dealing clearly with pensions was to be drawn up. A 'carefully worded letter' was to be sent to the British Medical Journal drawing attention to the fact that some private general practitioners did not make sufficient use of the District Nursing services for their elderly patients. This was the result of information from the District Nursing Associations that nurses were often called in too late and that the BMA, when the secretary of the Associations had written offering to collect concrete examples, had replied that it could not take up the matter at the moment. Doubtless, in wartime, the BMA had sufficient other preoccupations, but that apart, as was to be shown in other matters, its interest in social medicine did not match its interest in clinical medicine.

It is clear from the records that the day to day problems created by evacuation and war conditions generally kept the NOPW committee fully extended. The routine activities, it should perhaps be underlined, if only because the minutes make no mention of it, were being carried on in the constantly bombed capital of a country engaged in a war whose outcome, at that time, was in the balance, and which was not to end for another four years.

In that climate the committee turned its mind to post-war reconstruction and decided that Professor Holford, Minister of Works and Building, should be asked what plans, if any, were being made for the welfare of the old. He replied that he was prepared to consider a memorandum from the committee on housing schemes for old people. A Planning Sub-Committee was promptly appointed, which, within weeks, had invited for discussion a representative of PEP. It was he who suggested that the sub-committee should submit evidence to Sir William Beveridge's Committee, which was then sitting. Accordingly it widened its terms of reference to include housing with special application to the work of the Beveridge Committee, appointed an investigator to collate the material and even offered an honorarium of £50 for the job. When, a little later, Miss Keeling and Mrs Hill met Sir William Beveridge, they agreed that their inquiry should be directed rather to the special needs of old people than to the collection of general statistics. To look ahead a little, after receiving both written and oral evidence, the Beveridge Committee asked the OPWC for its considered views on two aspects of pensions. Should they be conditional on retirement from work – this to be considered from the point of view both of principle and administration – and at what age should they start in given circumstances? The OPWC could come to no firm conclusion on the second, and contented themselves with giving a summary of the various considerations which affected the question. They had no doubt whatsoever the contributory pensions should be paid at a fixed age, irrespective of retirement. At that time the complication of the 'earnings rule' was not introduced.

At the final meeting of its first full year's work, in December, 1941, the NOPWC accomplished a certain amount of reorganization which gave the Housing Sub-Committee more autonomy and Miss Keeling as secretary, Miss Samson replacing her as secretary of the main committee. Fresh matters were claiming the attention of the latter. A conference at the end of October had revealed the need for friendly visiting in their own homes of old people who missed their regular contact with the Relieving Officers, an often maligned group of people who, whatever the defects of the system which they had to administer, were personally regarded as friends by many of the old.

It was agreed that, as local OPW committees were formed, their attention should be drawn to this need for human contact. Other evidence coming in concerned the chronic sick. It was reported that some of the elderly who were discharged from hospital were too infirm to be taken into the homes which had been set up, which were neither staffed nor equipped for such residents.

So, in the first thirteen months after its founding, which have deliberately been treated in detail here, the new committee had not only put itself on the map, gained official recognition and extracted £2,000 from the pockets of a public which, at that time, might have been pardoned for showing little interest in problems so undramatic as those of the neglected old. It had already marked out for itself a field of work which, outside the difficulties peculiar to the state of war, remains valid today. It has been extended, but homes and housing, the adequacy of pensions, loneliness, the care of the chronic sick and infirm and the provision of proper medical treatment remain at the top of the NOPWC list of concerns today as they did twenty-five years ago.

CHAPTER IV

The First Years (1940-6)

By 1942, war, for Britain, had ceased to be an emergency and had become the norm. The mass raids and the problems they produced were over for the time being. Not until the coming of the rockets and flying bombs in the last year of hostilities was there once more provision for the evacuation of the elderly, as of children. To anticipate, when that time came, they went to Ministry of Health Hostels, none of which, when, in October, 1945, they were inspected on behalf of the NOPWC, were considered suitable as permanent homes for old people. In the meantime, life was bounded by makeshifts and material shortages which were to continue for some time after the end of the war, and the records of the NOPWC for these years reflect them.

In the first place, the old people themselves suffered directly from the shortages. Many of them had been accustomed to get such clothes as they needed at jumble sales and secondhand clothes stalls. Now, when the coupon system limited the number of new clothes which people could buy, supplies were down and prices were up. The committee followed its usual custom of collecting information from local branches which had now sprung up in fair numbers, discussed with the WVS the possibility of using for the needy old some of the clothes sent by the USA for war victims, and got from the NAB an assurance that, when necessary, it would give additional help, and, at need, extra coupons. There was concern also about the hardship suffered by many old people through the rationing of food and fuel.

They felt particularly the shortages of tea, eggs and milk and tobacco. Coal was not only scarce; it was difficult to get small quantities delivered and the old could seldom collect their own. While the country was facing a serious situation over the imports of food, it was hardly possible to press the Government to give special consideration to the elderly. The problem of coal

41

deliveries was more easily dealt with. Supplementary pensioners were already enabled to lay in a store of coal before winter by permission to draw their special allowances in advance. Now the NAB allowed this to be done monthly. British restaurants, which served solid, if not very meaty meals at reasonable prices, helped civilians through the rigours of rationing, but Miss Keeling suggested that perhaps meals centres with a club atmosphere would be more suitable for the old, who would possibly like also to be able to carry away a cooked meal to eat at home. Since the committee had available a sum of money which was a gift from Buenos Aires, it was agreed that a number of settlements and other bodies should be asked to consider opening experimental meals' centres. One such was opened at Bethnal Green by the Invalid Kitchens of London which was originally founded to provide meals for people whose condition demanded special diets. Before long the Bethnal Green Centre was serving 166 meals a week at 7d per head and considering an extension of its premises. Deptford, Marylebone, Lambeth, Paddington and Southwark followed the example. Soon twenty-five kitchens in the London area were serving half-portions of specially suitable dishes at reduced prices to old people. Woolwich went further and set up a mobile unit which took meals to housebound old people. So, in 1943, modestly enough, meals on wheels began.

Homes for old people continued to be a main subject of campaign by the NOPWC at this time. It had been estimated that, in December 1941, there were 630 old people in LCC hospitals and their base hospitals who, when ready for discharge seemed eligible for the NAB increased allowances which would enable them to enter a home, assuming that there was a home for them to enter.

When local voluntary societies established such homes, they had difficulty in getting equipment. There were various approaches to the ministries concerned. Miss Rathbone led a deputation of members to the Ministry of Health to talk about equipping homes. Miss Keeling and Mrs Margaret Neville Hill had an informal talk with Miss Florence Horsburgh, who stressed the great difficulty of finding staff and equipment and gave her own, unofficial view (there is little reason to suppose that it differed from any official view on the subject which may have existed then) that, in present conditions, the setting up of voluntary homes in any considerable number should not be attempted. She thought the Ministry of Health would be able to help in areas where there were insufficient vacancies in PAC institutions, and that voluntary homes might make more beds available by transferring senile cases to institutions. Another deputation to the Ministry of Health was at pains to point out that the kind of old person for whom the committee was anxious to encourage the setting up of homes was not that for which Public Assistance institutions traditionally catered, also that the aged sick for whom it was felt that voluntary homes were needed were not the same as the chronic sick cared for by the local authorities. The members of the deputation agreed to furnish particulars of actual cases which typified those for whom additional homes appeared to be needed.

Following all this, the NOPWC agreed that its Homes Sub-Committee should collect and collate the facts about the demand for places in homes and how far the existing provision, statutory and voluntary, was able to meet the need, then frame proposals based on the information gathered. But even before it started it was clear that Miss Horsburgh's view was at variance with that of the growing number of people up and down the country who were concerned with the welfare of the old. Various local committees were preoccupied with the matter.

Liverpool, looking ahead, suggested that war memorials might take the form of old people's homes. The branch urged at the same time that the national committee should press for a change in legislation to ensure that pensions should be paid direct to old people in institutions, who could then pay their weekly fees and keep the balance as they would do in a voluntary home. As early as 1944 the Friends' Relief Service wished to ask the NAB whether, with supplementary pension increased, there could be an increase to bring the income of those in approved homes to more than 30s weekly, also that classification of those eligible for it should be widened from 'those receiving special care and attention' to 'those unable to care adequately for themselves'. It was pointed out that when the NAB had originally fixed the sum at 30s it was on the basis that some of the costs of voluntary homes came from their own funds. The

Church Army homes, for instance, paid no rent for their premises, and so could manage tolerably well on the basis of 30s per head per week. As more public utility societies came into existence, whose homes would have to be entirely self-supporting, it might be necessary for the Board to reconsider the situation. The battle to obtain an adequate system of registration of homes went on, and the committee welcomed a resolution from the County Councils Association, calling for new legislation requiring registration, with its consequent implications, of 'homes which receive for gain people suffering from infirmities from age or from other causes'. This was to be a persistent problem, one of the difficulties being that of evolving a definition for a home for the infirm aged which would distinguish it clearly from a hospital. Until October, 1944, the Housing and Homes Sub-Committee continued to carry on the work of placing old people in homes, then, for an experimental period of one year, the Charity Organizations Society took over the task. A few months earlier the NOPWC had become an autonomous body, for which the NCSS still provided finance and a secretariat, also some special services. Its resources were fully stretched and to be able to hand over to a competent body the important but time-consuming job of placing must have been a considerable relief.

The other major interest in these years was housing for the old, since, obviously, the number of homes needed was linked with the number of suitable houses which were available. Talks with the Registrar of Friendly Societies and the National Federation of Housing Societies revealed that it was comparatively simple for an existing housing society to become a public utility society, or for a new society to be formed for that purpose, and that model rules drawn up by the NFHS for use by housing associations would serve equally well for public utility societies. Local authorities were empowered to lend up to 90 per cent of the value of a house when reconditioned, and there were promising experiments also in which a local authority took over large, old houses, fitted them as bedsitting-rooms and handed over to a voluntary society responsibility for rent collecting and for the general welfare of the residents. The Church Army was prepared to buy and maintain houses which would be converted into bedsitting-rooms with cooking facilities for the able-bodied

44

elderly. Preston formed a Housing Association to provide quarters for old people on a higher income level. The City Parochial Charities, in a building scheme at Islington, planned forty dwellings for old people who could take their main meal of the day in a common dining-room and, when they were ill, went into a sick bay which was permanently staffed. So, before the end of hostilities, the prototypes of what are today's commonplaces in the housing of old people came into being.

Clubs, too, were multiplying, encouraged by the statement of the Minister of Health in 1945 that he was prepared to entertain applications from County and County Borough Councils for the payment of annual grants towards the support and maintenance of Old People's Clubs. Here and there local authorities were taking over responsibilities for Home Help schemes which had been established by voluntary societies and which had proved second only to the District Nursing service in value to old people.

When so much was being accomplished it was hard for the committee, in 1944, to read an article in the *Daily Sketch* lamenting the lack of any organization caring for the old. The chairman wrote to set the record straight, and, in the following year, the publication of Miss Samson's book on the work of the committee, *Old Age in the New World*, made it known to a wider public. The first edition of 6,000 was quickly sold out. A second edition was impossible without a special allocation of paper; it had to wait until, rather unexpectedly, the RAF Education Department ordered 3,000 copies of the book and supplied their own paper. In fact, a second organization concerned with the welfare of the aged was coming to birth. The Nuffield Foundation was about to implement the fifth objective of its constitution, which was 'the care and comfort of the aged', by setting up the National Corporation for the Care of Old People. Immediately, since the National Corporation was a grant-distributing body, the NOPWC had it to thank for an annual contribution which was welcome indeed at a time when its finances were still pitiably straitened. In the long run its 'higher mandarin' function in experiment, research, criticism and policy-making are likely to be seen as the more valuable half of its work, of which more will be heard later in this book.

At this time the NOPWC was eager to broaden the basis of its

45

membership to make it more representative of those which it was trying to serve. Bodies like the TUC and the Miners' Welfare Funds were approached before they themselves felt eager to join; the committee, clearly, did not wish to set into the image of members of the professional classes doing good to the less fortunate. It is interesting to note in passing that when, a few years later, the question of medical representation arose, the members felt that neither the BMA nor the Medical Society for the Care of the Elderly were suitable bodies to be represented. They decided finally that the most suitable medical member would be Lord Amulree, then President of the Medical Society for the Care of the Elderly.

In the day to day work of the committee the end of the war, in the summer of 1945, made little difference. Shortages continued, the familiar problems persisted. The notable date, for several reasons, was 1946, which, looking back, can be seen to mark the end of the initial phase of the NOPWC's existence.

In that year, with the death of Eleanor Rathbone on January 2, the committee lost a chairman who was one of the most distinguished personalities of her time and a constant inspiration to any social work enterprise. 'She was,' writes Mr John Moss, who served as her vice-chairman, 'a remarkable woman. She had shown her concern with the poor and needy since her early days, when, upon leaving the university, she undertook a factual inquiry into the position of widows under the Poor Law. Although she is remembered chiefly as a Member of Parliament, and for her advocacy of family allowances, those who knew her realized her interest in all aspects of social welfare. This was why she responded so readily to the request that she should become our first chairman. She had tireless energy and sensitivity to human suffering, and, throughout her life, acted on the axiom that "whatever ought to be done can be done".'

Her successor was her complement rather than her obverse. Eleanor Rathbone typified that Victorian and Edwardian professional class from which Britain drew the greater number of its pioneer social workers. Mr Fred Messer, M.P., started with a more intimate knowledge of those whom social workers set out to serve. At a time when the National Assistance Act was on the horizon, it is difficult to imagine anyone better fitted to pilot the committee through an epoch of radical change. His vice-chairman, Mr John Moss, was one of the rare workers who had one foot in the statutory and one in the voluntary field. As Public Assistance Officer for Kent he knew the best and the worst of the system which was shortly to be superseded, and he knew also how great was the need that voluntary work should continue in the Welfare State.

In 1946, also, the NOPWC organized its first public conference, held at Conway Hall, London, on November 29 and 30. In the sense that no resolutions were passed, it was not a policy-making event. It was called to secure public discussion of the many problems which faced the committee in its daily work and to make known its aims and needs to a wider circle. It attracted 427 delegates, of whom 160 came from Government departments and local authorities, the rest from voluntary organizations. Twenty years later the report of the proceedings is a valuable record of how much had been accomplished in seven years.

It showed the real concern of the Assistance Board for the problems of the old, brought, from the late Dr Marjory Warren, of the West Middlesex Hospital, what, for many, must have been the first account they had heard of the possibilities of geriatric medicine, and emphasized a problem which is still with us – the need for a proper liaison between the hospital and home provision for the elderly sick, not to say the absence, also still with us, of anything like adequate provision for the elderly infirm. Also, in Mr James Griffiths, Minister of National Insurance, who gave the opening address, it had the herald of the brave new world whose building had started four years earlier, with the publication of the Beveridge Report, continued with the passing of the Family Allowances Act, the Industrial Injuries Act, the National Insurance Act and the National Health Service Act. In that year, incidentally, the rate of retirement pension for contributory pensioners was 26s for a single person, 42s for a married couple, who, said Mr Griffiths, would be permitted to earn up to 20s a week each without their pension being affected.

The Minister was naturally proud of the Government's achievement. What made his speech remarkable was that, nevertheless, he acknowledged that there were some aspects in the lives of the old which legislation was powerless to transform.

Speaking of the 65,000 old age pensioners over eighty years of age, and the 200,000 old couples over seventy who were, at that time, living on their own, Mr Griffiths said: 'Here is a problem in this Britain of ours which, proud as I am of this Act, I know money cannot solve – the tremendous problem of loneliness in old age. I hope therefore that there will be an expansion of this work. In some ways it becomes more urgent and more important now that we have brought in this new Act. I am sure that we can leave it – and I leave it with confidence – to those who are represented here and the organizations through which you work.'

He went on to voice what should be the perennial guiding principle in work for the old: 'I would like to emphasize one thing here which I think should be the right approach for all of us. It would be doing no real service to the aged people if a tendency were to grow up to regard their problems in isolation from the rest of the community. I think it would certainly be a very great pity if any kind of antagonism grew up between the needs of the old people and those of the younger generation. It is not a real service to old people to try and isolate them, either in their homes or from the rest of the community. Their greatest pleasure is that, though old, they are an essential part of the community, a part of the neighbourhood.'

Mr (now Sir Harold) H. Fieldhouse, Secretary of the Assistance Board, took up the same theme. Old people were not a class apart. Like everyone else they needed, first of all, an income which was sufficient to prevent their being in financial want; like everyone else they needed suitable houses or other accommodation; and like everyone else they had their worries and troubles. They differed as a class from the rest of the community as regards their requirements in the last two categories only in degree and because so many of them could not cope with their difficulties unaided. And, on less tangible problems: 'A moderate income and shelter over their heads do not absolve old people from the worries and troubles of life. Loneliness, boredom, increasing infirmity, were magnified into almost over-whelming problems, which to younger people might be merely minor irritation.' Mr Fieldhouse was adamant that friendly visiting of lonely old people was a job for the voluntary worker. It would be unreasonable to expect the tax-payer to pay an official to go round and visit old people and talk about their interests. It was obvious that he made a clear separation between such visits and the welfare service which the Assistance Board would still be empowered to provide even after the new pension became payable.

Even at that early stage the NOPWC did not make such a division: it was hoped that friendly visitors would keep their eyes and ears open for difficulties when they were in the homes of the old, and, when necessary, would get in touch with the appropriate service. There was no suggestion, however, that Mr Fieldhouse denigrated voluntary workers. Not only did he look forward to their continued and increasing help, he realized that a great deal of thought and discrimination was necessary in selecting them, while hoping at the same time that 'technical efficiency will not be allowed to push into the background the first requirement of a social worker, which is a natural and genuine liking of people'.

The rest of the conference was technical in the sense that the speakers were skilled in fields other than administration – the blend of exhortation and expertise was one which was to prove its worth at later conferences. On this occasion it gave a platform to Dr Marjory Warren, Deputy Medical Director to the West Middlesex County Hospital, who had been accomplishing a quiet revolution among the aged sick in what had been a typical workhouse infirmary. Today, when we accept as a commonplace that geriatric medicine can get old people out of bed and onto their legs after long term illnesses, even if, too often, we have no idea what to do with them once they are mobile again, it is difficult to realize the astonishment with which the ideas of the few pioneers like herself were received. It is not unfair to say that in the opinion of large numbers of doctors, let alone lay people, all that one could hope to do for old people who had to go into hospital was to keep them clean and if possible free from bedsores. Dr Warren, practically, pointed out that if the elderly in hospital were 'left untreated until they became untreatable', hospitals would fairly quickly silt up. Her own plan included a team of medical, nursing and social workers which is even today rare enough, more research into the diseases of old age and – which, in the light of later events was painfully apposite – the unification of the authorities caring for the aged sick and for the aged who needed hostel accommodation.

The NOPWC's workers had already had cause to know that 'in advanced age it is indeed a fine line between sickness and infirmity not amounting to sickness', and, before long, they were to devote a great deal of energy to pleading with the authorities for easier transfer from hospital to old people's home, and vice versa.

At the conference Dr Warren was backed up by the late Sir Ernest Rock Carling, the eminent surgeon noted for his concern for the welfare of the elderly, who said she had shown that, out of every 100 patients lying in Public Assistance Institutions, twenty-five could be got upon their feet again in a condition to fend for themselves. But he put the crux of the problem when he said if it was difficult to get the elderly into hospital, it was even more difficult, when they were cured or recovered, to get them into any home conditions really suitable for them. Sir Ernest, like Dorothy Keeling years before him, was conscious of the deep unhappiness which the total want of occupation could cause to the old, and the NOPWC had provided against this, too, by including in the programme a talk by Miss E. Lyth, formerly Welfare Officer to the Surrey County Council under the evacuation scheme, who had spent the six years of war devising occupational interests for aged persons. If, today, our hearts do not immediately leap at the idea of threading beads made from sealing-wax or gold or silver paper, turning old straw hats into tea cosies and old felt ones into posies and making afternoon jackets from old blackout curtains, we should project ourselves back into that period of wartime and post-war frugality when almost anything which was not strictly necessary could be a source of pleasure and relief. Hessian traycloths and raffia treasure boxes were among the few outlets available to a would-be consumer society, and, in fairness, Miss Lyth's talk ranged from the importance of a library service and attractive hairstyles for old ladies to the keeping up of birthday celebrations and the saving of the price of a dog licence by putting twopenny stamps on a card each week. During the discussion it emerged that the LCC provided cookery teachers to go to old people, an idea which even today is probably not sufficiently widespread.

Finally, an architect, Mr Edward Armstrong, gave an account of homes for old people in Scandinavia. We still have some cause to feel envious of the Danish system of three general categories of homes for the old, catering, respectively, for those who were still able-bodied and independent, those who were frail and intermittently ill and those who needed constant help and attention. In 1946, for an audience in Britain which was interested in the subject, and might fairly think of itself as progressive, to learn that, in Denmark and Sweden, there was no restriction as to clothing in any type of old people's home, that the whole atmosphere was as little institutional as possible and that, except in the hospital section of the homes, the tenants were encouraged to have their own furniture, if not too cumbersome, and their own pictures, photographs and curtains must have been startling indeed.

Later conferences organized by the NOPWC were to give more time to discussion, and, often, to pass resolutions on some currently urgent topic. This first one was more concerned with making known the aims, and even the existence, of an organization concerned with the welfare of the old, and with encouraging the establishing of local committees up and down the country. It served both purposes at a time when the coming major changes in legislation made it particularly desirable that some independent body should hold a watching brief on behalf of those who were to be affected by it.

CHAPTER V

The Problem of Legislation

It is generally true that voluntary organizations seldom influence directly the character of social legislation. Typically, their rôle is to create a climate of public opinion which leads to legislation, or to help to make acceptable legislation which may be slightly ahead of at least some sections of public opinion. An obvious example of the first is the early work of the associations concerned with maternity and child welfare, of the second, the educational campaign which accompanied the Mental Health Act (1959), with its emphasis on the community care of the mentally ill.

There are exceptions, one of which was the NOPWC's contribution to the framing of the National Assistance Act (1948). It was at this time strategically particularly well placed to do so, since its chairman, Mr Fred (now Sir Fred) Messer, was not only a Member of Parliament and Chairman of the Central Health Services' Committee, but also Vice-Chairman of the Middlesex County Health Committee, and so was in a position to take a well rounded view of the problems of the old and their possible remedy. Through him the committee was constantly in touch with the Ministry during the time the Bill was being prepared. Of one of its provisions it could claim authorship. It was as a direct result of pressure by the NOPWC that, at the Report stage of the Bill, the Minister himself proposed an amendment including country district councils among the local authorities empowered to contribute to clubs and meals' services for old people. The underlying principle here was the sound one that it was often the small authority which had the greatest interest and possibly the most intimate knowledge of those problems. But throughout the committee stages the Ministry was kept aware of the view of voluntary bodies. Mr Messer was later to say that the Bill became a better Act because of amendments suggested by the NOPWC.

The next six years were to be particularly eventful, whether in the development of new services for the old, the introduction of new legislation affecting them or the acute growing pains associated with the beginnings of the Welfare State and particularly with the NHS Act. Fairly early on in the period the Minister of Health was on record as saying that: 'No matter what provision we make there will always be a place for voluntary organizations. For only by voluntary organization are you able to touch the bottomless reservoir of kindness, humanity and self-sacrifice.' He and his colleagues were to discover also the vigorous and informed criticism which would come from the NOPWC, for the first three years under the chairmanship of Mr Messer, for the second under that of Mr John Moss, also rarely qualified in that he represented both statutory and voluntary interests. For the committee this era was one in which it was more actively involved in political campaigning (which, it need hardly be said, does not imply party political) than at any time in its existence. It was an exacting, and in some ways a frustrating exercise, but it was not without reward. When, in August, 1954, forty-two countries were represented at the International Gerontological Congress held at Church House, Westminster, they paid tribute to the 'comprehensive way in which Britain is trying to meet the needs of the old, which is not achieved to the same extent in any other country'.

To return to the National Assistance Act, it offered almost unlimited possibilities of co-operation between voluntary and statutory services. Local authorities were empowered to provide certain services through voluntary organizations, which they might either subsidize or employ as their agents. Obviously, it was to the advantage of local authorities to make use of voluntary associations which were already providing satisfactory services and to co-ordinate their own work with them. It was not a question of resources only – and here the combined efforts of both parties could scarcely meet the existing needs – but of knowledge and experience.

In many departments of welfare and social work the trailblazing in Britain had been done by voluntary agencies, and their expertise could be most valuable to local authorities in preparing their own schemes. The Minister was being no more than practical when he strongly recommended that the two sides should confer.

The section of the Act which placed on County and County Boroughs the duty to provide residential accommodation for persons who 'by reason of age, infirmity or other circumstances' were in need of care and attention not otherwise available to them stipulated that 'it should be available to all who needed it, irrespective of their means, but that it should be paid for in accordance with resources'. It permitted arrangements between local authorities and voluntary organizations for the provision of accommodation, with general power to contribute to the funds of voluntary bodies which provided, or proposed to provide such accommodation, and this covered housing associations. The last was particularly important. Under the Act, a housing association could obtain help from both the local authority and from the Exchequer, so the NOPWC urged local committees to form them. The need was acute, a Bulletin of the period wrote: 'Unless voluntary organizations continue to work with enthusiasm to establish more homes, not nearly enough accommodation will be provided for old people who need communal care, e.g. in the London and Greater London area, only 8·5 per cent of those old people who are known to want this care can today obtain vacancies (it should not be assumed that, in this, London and Greater London were typical of the rest of the country).'

Another section of the Act allowed all local authorities to make contributions to the funds of any voluntary organization, and here again the Minister hoped they would use this power to foster 'the excellent work of this kind being done by voluntary bodies in many areas'. At a time when clubs for old people were rapidly increasing in number, and when local schemes included those for meals, home helps, chiropody and laundry, to name but a few, the possibilities offered here were exhilarating.

Almost immediately the appropriate sub-committee of the Central Housing Advisory Committee of the Ministry of Health invited the NOPWC to submit a memorandum on housing for old people. It is worth reproducing fully, partly as evidence of how relatively advanced was the thinking of the committee twenty years ago, and, more painfully, as a reminder that even now not all its recommendations have come into effect. Starting with the obvious truth that there was not at that time enough accommodation being provided for old people, and that unless

54

this was rectified the problem would become increasingly serious because of the rising proportion of old people in the population, the committee pressed for more effective liaison between housing authorities and welfare authorities, when these were different bodies. It cited as an example of the situations which could result when it did not exist a housing estate on which old people's dwellings of excellent design were being built. But there seemed no link with, or even knowledge of the county council's plans for providing accommodation for old people in need of care, though the two were obviously inter-dependent.

The memorandum went on to suggest that space might be reserved on housing estates for the building of old people's homes when permits could be allowed (this, it should be remembered, was a period of strict controls on building), and that local authorities, when acquiring existing property for use as residential accommodation, should pay particular attention to the present and future needs of old people housed in the area. It was desirable for each resident in an old people's home to have his or her own bedsitting-room and to be allowed to furnish it with at least some of their own possessions (it conceded that some of the very frail and very old might prefer a shared room, a view which still has support today).

It was thought that, on housing estates, a canteen or restaurant might be helpful, though, unless this was in addition to ordinary rations, old people would not make use of it. There seems no record of this idea ever having been put into practice, but, even today, it appears to have possibilities, perhaps as an adjunct to Meals on Wheels. Rather surprisingly, the memorandum did not think there was any general desire for a communal laundry on estates, though this was before the days of launderettes. It stressed the desirability of somebody's being in frequent contact with old people who lived alone. This was not necessarily a job for a professional. It could be done by a caretaker with a small salary, or simply by a friendly person who would make it her business to see that doctor, home help, district nurse, or whatever other help was needed, was found quickly. On material details it thought that extra bedrooms on an estate for the temporary use of visiting relatives or friends would be much appreciated. If old people were housed above the first storey lifts were not merely desirable, they were essential. In the planning of bathrooms there was room for experiment with foot baths and 'sitz' baths; in the planning of kitchens it was worth remembering that most old people preferred gas to electricity for cooking, if only because it was what they were used to. The old should have the opportunity of renting an allotment if they so wished, and – most practically – seats between an old people's home and the shopping centre would be helpful.

Housing associations were on the programme of that year's national conference, the third to be organized by the NOPWC, which was held at the Friends' House, London, on November 26 and 27, 1948. The general theme was Problems and Progress in Old People's Welfare, and there was progress to report as well as advice to be given on visiting, clubs for old people and various meals services, in addition to the work of housing associations for old people, which was dealt with by Miss M. Merrylees, Secretary, the National Federation of Housing Societies. The outstanding problem was one which had been broached at the previous national conference and, for some years, was to be a major preoccupation of the committee, the care of the aged sick, who were not necessarily synonymous with the chronic sick.

In fairness, this was not a problem which had been created by the new Health Service, though, certainly, it had been made very much worse by the division of responsibility between health and welfare authorities. As early at 1941 the NOPWC had received complaints that some old people discharged from hospital were still too infirm to be taken into such homes as were available to them, and at this stage there was a clear realization in the minds of the members, if not always in the mind of authority, that there was a distinction between the aged sick and the chronic sick. In March, 1945, there had been an approach to the Minister of Health about the 'impossibility' of finding accommodation for the aged and sick in institutions, 'particularly in Suffolk'. In 1946 the committee sent a resolution to the Ministry, expressing its concern over the shortage of hospital beds for the old and drawing attention to the difficulty often experienced by those who were running voluntary homes in transferring to hospital old people who were sufficiently ill to need full nursing care. It had been in touch with the BMA, which had a long-term policy to meet the situation – it was concerned that old people's homes should not establish sick bays for the permanent care of sick old people. The committee, which had itself been pressing the need for hospital treatment, as opposed to mere hospital or institutional care for such of the old as need it, agreed, but more practically wanted to know what was to happen to the old people in the meantime. Indeed, Dr Grieg Anderson, Chairman of the BMA Committee on the Care and Treatment of the Elderly and Infirm, who had addressed the NOPWC's second national conference in November, 1947, had admitted that the scheme outlined in the booklet it had prepared, *The Care and Treatment of the Elderly Infirm*, was 'in many ways ideal, or even idealistic', and that it would be 'many years' before it could be made completely effective and efficient.

The position had become more acutely difficult when the new Acts came into force because the Relieving Officer no longer had the power to order a hospital to take in an old person who was ill and uncared for, as he had been able to do with the former Public Assistance infirmaries. Admittedly, there may have been times when all that could be offered the patient was a bed hastily put up in a corridor and such care as an over-burdened nursing staff could manage, but at least he or she was not left totally alone and untended.

The conference was given some idea of the size of the problem by Dr Trevor Howell, of St John's Hospital Battersea, who used in illustration the pensioners of the Royal Hospital, Chelsea. Despite the fact that they were a picked body of healthy old men, with admirable surroundings and every care, one third of them were admitted to the Infirmary of the Hospital every year. Admittedly, old people living at home would not go into hospital for minor ailments, but the neglect of minor ailments was liable to lead to more serious conditions later, and, at present, there were old people who failed to find a doctor who could, or would, take them on his list. Others, more fortunate, found that the doctor could not give the time and attention they really needed. When he could, it might still be impossible to obtain necessary treatment. General hospitals did not like to admit elderly patients because they wished to use scarce resources to the best effect. He quoted here the example of eight old men suffering chronic diseases occupying beds in a surgical ward. On a reasonable calculation, their presence over a long period had prevented about 280 acutely ill patients from receiving treatment. Sometimes, again, even when elderly patients could be discharged, there was nowhere suitable for them to go. Six of his own patients, each of whom had had strokes, had, by careful treatment and rehabilitation been brought to the point when, at least they could look after themselves. But if they were discharged, one would have to live alone in a second-storey flat, another at the top of a converted house with no indoor sanitation and so on. The obvious answer was that they should go into a home or an institution, but he found it almost impossible to persuade any of his patients to enter an institution, while old people's homes either had long waiting lists or would take only the healthy. He believed that if a regular two-way traffic could be established between hospitals and homes it would solve some of the problems of both.

The discussion after Dr Howell's address revealed how widespread concern was about the situation. Already the committee had written to the Ministry pointing out that, since July, 1948, some teaching hospitals no longer had beds for old people who needed treatment, and suggesting that all should accept a definite proportion—perhaps 10 per cent—of such patients. Also there should be arrangements for the transfer to old people's homes of the non-sick aged who were at present occupying hospital beds. At present the shortage of district nurses and their often unsuitable housing conditions made the position of those who were ill at home especially unfortunate. This letter referred also to the BMA's publication, *The Right Patient in the Right Bed*, which had recommended a co-ordinated service in selected general hospitals for the better investigation and treatment of diseases and disability in old people, which would work in conjunction with long-stay annexes for irremediable patients and residential homes for those needing only domestic care.

Now the committee decided to send to the Minister the resolution passed at the conference, which had pointed the 'dire urgency' of the problem and pressed the desirability of special accommodation being made available for old people in all training hospitals, so ensuring that this branch of nursing was part of a nurse's training. By July, 1949, Mr Messer and Lord Amulree, the first medical member of the NOPWC, jointly felt that something should be done administratively or legislatively, to settle the problem of definition of responsibility between health and welfare authorities, which was the cause of much suffering to that large class of old people who had been described as 'neither ill enough to be in hospital nor well enough to be in a home'. In practice, they fluctuated between tolerable health, or, at least, wellbeing, and sudden, acute illness, and the list of those who died, in greater or less misery, while administrative wrangling over their proper destination continued, was lengthening.

A memorandum on the subject went from the NOPWC to the NAB and to the Minister of Health. It produced a reply from the Minister, who 'fully realized' the difficulties which had arisen, and welcomed 'so warmly' a projected experiment by the King Edward's Hospital Fund and the National Corporation for the Care of Old People in providing special annexes in which there would be a degree of nursing care. But he doubted whether he could agree to a suggestion that a new statutory body was required which would fuse the interests of the Regional Hospital Board and the Local Health Authority. This might be 'a retrograde step'. One of the main jobs in dealing with the aged had been to get the different classes sorted out and accommodated in institutions suitable to their particular needs, and with this in mind it was broadly right that sick and non-sick persons should be looked after by different bodies. It would not be a solution to go back and lump all old people together as under the Poor Law. The problem needed much further study.

As a statement this bears all the marks of bad Civil Service thinking and Ministerial lack of logic, with the lot shoved into the 'Pending' basket at the end, but some allowance must be made for the weight of history. The Poor Law was part of the national folk lore; the Poor Law infirmary, as it had existed for generations, was, medically speaking, a horror which no thinking doctor could wish to have perpetuated. It remains unfortunate that the perfectly understandable attitude which resulted should have hindered temporary measures which might at that time have done something to alleviate the lot of many sick old people. One which, about this time, did help to bring relief to families, if only on a small scale, was the setting up, here and there, of schemes for 'night-sitters', that is, women, usually not nurses, who would take over for an occasional night to give

59

some relief to the family of an elderly invalid, or care for a solitary one.

The campaign continued through 1950. In February of that year the Minister of Health had acknowledged the value of voluntary social work for the old by sending out a circular (11/50) asking local authorities to support and encourage the establishment of Old People's Welfare Committees where they did not yet exist, and emphasizing the value of an exchange of information between the local authorities and voluntary bodies. Its results were dramatic. Mr F. S. Wilkinson, then Under-Secretary to the Ministry of Health, personally gave a great deal of assistance with the work of co-ordinating OPW committees. In the space of roughly two years their number rose from 378 to 831. Undoubtedly their efficiency as well as their size and scope was extremely uneven, but, at worst, a local committee was a focus for interest in and a centre for the spreading information about the needs of old people. The circular stressed also that it was important to create a voluntary home visiting scheme – this was a theme upon which Mr James Griffiths had spoken in the House of Commons a year or so earlier. The national committee was grateful, and, obviously, delighted also when, in June, 1950, there was a debate on Old People's Welfare in the House in which Mr Messer took part. But the problem of hospital beds remained intransigent. In the summer of 1950 a deputation from the NOPWC waited upon the Minister. It was a notably well-informed one. The chairman, Mr Messer, had experience as Chairman of the Central Health Services' Council and Chairman of a Regional Hospital Board. Dr E. B. Brooke was a geriatrician whose hospital, St Helier, Carshalton, Surrey, specialized in domiciliary care. Miss Lamb represented the nursing profession, and Miss D. Ramsey, secretary of the NOPWC, apart from her overall familiarity with the subject, had, a short time before, been at the receiving end of reports from twenty-three working parties set up by Old People's Welfare Committees in various parts of the country to consider the situation in their districts.

The Minister's last communication on the subject with the committee had been in reply to a suggestion of the need for somebody in the position of the Relieving Officer, with his powers to ensure hospital admission. He had said then that he did not think the statutory approach of entitling an officer to give an order for the admission of a person to an establishment was the right way. He did not want the hospital authorities to be responsible for those who were not sick. The problem had been 'partly created by the success of the social services'. Originally old people lived more generally with their children. The break-up of the human family was the real reason for some difficulties. The Home Help Service was very expensive; they must try to bring the relative back into the picture in another way'. There was 'no effective substitute for the good neighbour', and there must be more voluntary visiting. Behind the comfortable mythology of a good deal of this – many needy old people, for instance, had no children with whom they could live, or had children who, with families, were crowded into a three-roomed flat – lay, of course, the truth that, at that period, it was impossible to coax from the Treasury more money for services for old people. It is never easy. The view expressed by an American politician, 'Geriatrics are OK, but they aren't a growth industry' is widely held.

Now, face to face, the deputation presented a considered memorandum on the subject. The old who were suffering from the inability of the Regional Hospital Boards to provide beds, it stated, fell into two categories, those who were in acute need of treatment, and so were acute cases, irrespective of age, and those in pain which could be alleviated by hospital care, although perhaps no permanent improvement could be anticipated. Beds were unavailable partly because of the shortage of nurses and of other hospital services, but partly because many were blocked by old people who no longer needed hospital treatment and who, if suitable accommodation were available, could be transferred immediately. Some of these could return to their relatives if there were more domiciliary help. Others had no relatives, and were too frail for the average Party III establishment (that is, a local authority Welfare Department home).

The reference to transfers here was not theoretical. At St Helier Hospital, eight patients who, between them, had been occupying beds continuously for three and a quarter years, had been successfully transferred to more suitable accommodation in a nursing home for old people. This was the special home run by Field Lane Institution in co-operation with the hospital.

It can claim to have been the first 'half-way' home ever established. In its setting up Dr Brooke, one of the great names in geriatric medicine, was fortunate in finding at the head of Field Lane the Revd H. J. White under whose leadership the institution did enlightened work for the elderly.

The deputation's memorandum went on to point out the difficulty of determining whether the Regional Hospital Board was responsible for a patient when the condition of an old person was liable to fluctuate from one week, or even from one day to the next. It was obviously impractical to think of transferring them back and forth from hospital to home, even if hospital accommodation were available. The members stressed to the Minister that some procedure should be recommended by which, on medical advice, responsibility for the maintenance of a particular person on transfer should be agreed.

At present old people in their own homes were suffering because they were falling between two stools of responsibility. They needed urgently some kind of care, but often there was administrative difficulty in determining the proper responsible authority, which led to lengthy arguments, during which the old person remained at home, inadequately cared for, unless he or she resolved the problem by dying. There was a shortage not only of home nurses and home helps, but of money to pay for them. Some local authorities which would have no difficulty in finding more home helps would not extend their service because of extra cost to the rates. But, said the members of the deputation, since home care cost less than hospital care, and since it was easier to find home helps than nurses, there was a good economic case for extending both the home help service and the number of old people's homes by sharing the cost between the local authority and the national exchequer. It was important also to make it readily possible for a sick patient in an old people's home to be admitted to hospital, or there was danger of homes developing into the old type of Poor Law Infirmary, with inadequate nursing. Voluntary bodies might be increasingly reluctant to accept the responsibility of establishing homes unless they were sure that there would be a hospital bed for a patient who was in need of treatment.

Could the Hospital Management Committees be induced not to work in watertight compartments, and to cross boundaries when it was convenient, asked the deputation? Could they not let local authorities use empty wards in hospitals, which could not be used for patients because of the shortage of nurses, but which could be used by and staffed for the care of old people who were not sick but needed only care and attention?

The Minister was still convinced that there was 'no administrative lacuna' (he is quoted as using this dreadful phrase) but promised to consider the points raised in the memorandum. He gave the useful reminder that domiciliary services, like laundry for incontinent old people, could now be dealt with by Housing Authorities under the new powers conferred by the 1949 Act. Otherwise he could only urge that everything possible should be done to prevent the old from becoming bedridden.

There was no immediate solution, no easy happy ending to this campaign. Proper provision for the elderly infirm remains today one of the least satisfactory areas of care for the old; only in the care of the mentally frail is the situation more worrying. Right through the years to the mid-nineteen-fifties the committee battled, aided occasionally by press publicity of particularly scandalous situations. They urged on the Minister that when there was any doubt about who was responsible for any elderly patient there should always be joint consultation, and that, if there could be no immediate agreement, one person should be responsible for deciding on the immediate placing of an elderly patient needing hospital treatment or care and shelter, leaving any difference of opinion to be settled later. Some regions did in fact appoint a medical referee with this power, but these were purely local arrangements, the fruits of that goodwill between Regional Hospital Board and local authority which the Minister, on another occasion, said was 'the only thing needed to make sure that everybody was catered for'. (The deputation involved in this meeting replied rather tartly that, in some areas, goodwill did not exist, and local groups looked to the Ministry for guidance in dealing with borderline cases.) In fact, there was no money, and therefore no foreseeable hope of a substantial increase in the provision of any of the necessary services. The Minister spoke the plain truth when, in a letter to the committee in the summer of 1953, he repeated an assurance given in the House of Commons by his Parliamentary Secretary that 'the Government fully recognized the importance and urgency of the care of the aged, and was concerned to see that all steps were taken within the limits of capital resources, maintenance expenditure and manpower that can be devoted to this one aspect of the social service, to ensure that the sick and aged are given every care and attention'.

In such a situation the constant and active concern of the NOPWC was more than ever necessary. It approached the Ministry, not with emotional appeals, but with well-documented briefs. By now, ten years or so after its founding, it could call on every department of expertise involved in the care of the old; through its local branches it knew what was really happening at ground level. Certainly it can claim credit for the ameliorative measures that were gradually introduced – more 'night sitter' schemes, more arrangements for doing, within twenty-four hours, the laundry of the incontinent old. Early in 1953, there was a small triumph towards which the NOPWC had undoubtedly contributed, though it was not directly involved in the event. In March of that year the Minister wrote to the Lord Mayor of Birmingham ruling that the City Council could very properly accept responsibility for the provision and maintenance of necessary accommodation under Part III of the National Assistance Act for the frail elderly needing constant nursing. There must be close liaison between the Regional Hospital Board and the local authority in dealing with borderline cases. This was the first time the National Committee had heard of a local authority in England (there was already one – Glasgow – in Scotland) which, after discussion with the Ministry, had decided to set up a home for those needing more than average care and attention though they did not need hospital treatment. It was at pains to spread the news in the hope that others might be similarly inspired.

This whole episode is a model of the way in which an efficient voluntary organization can at once keep Government constantly aware of the degree to which its services are falling short and also help local authorities with their current difficulties. It is notable also that, preoccupied as the committee was with short-term emergency measures, it never ceased to hold before the Ministry the long-term remedies for a situation which perhaps, financial crisis or no, might have been tackled with a greater sense of urgency if politicians and senior civil servants had been despatched on a few rounds among the aged and also often impoverished sick under the guidance of selected District Nurses and general practitioners. It might still be a salutary exercise today, with visits to a few of our less laudable geriatric and psycho-geriatric wards thrown in.

CHAPTER VI

The aims and policy
of the NOPWC

Mr Messer resigned the chairmanship of the National Committee, while retaining his interest in its work, in 1951, and was succeeded by his vice-chairman, Mr John Moss. His going was regretted by all who had worked with him. To succeed Eleanor Rathbone in office might have been a daunting prospect for anyone, and the committee had given the matter much thought and heart-searching before deciding to approach Mr Messer. They never had any doubts of the rightness of their choice. Apart from his wide experience in social welfare he had an immediate friendliness and approachability which made him universally liked.

In the following year, 1952, Miss Dorothea Ramsey, who had succeeded Miss Keeling as secretary and had held the post for seven years, also resigned, to be succeeded in her turn by Miss Marjorie Bucke, the present secretary. One of Miss Ramsey's last enterprises had been to make a three months' tour of America, returning to report of old people's work there, as do travellers reporting on other departments of life in the USA, that it was 'so like and so unlike'. Strong pressure groups were bringing together those over sixty-five years old, so that financial provision for old people was a political issue. There was little voluntary work in the county homes for the old and a great difference in atmosphere between the official and the voluntary homes. America felt that the old should, as far as possible, remain in their own homes, but, as yet, there was almost no housing intended for the elderly, or, indeed, much housing suitable for single people of any age. There was little voluntary visiting, and it was doubted whether it could be done by non-professionals. The club movement for old people was spreading and there was one development which had yet to reach Britain.

At Ann Arbor, University of Michigan, also two public libraries in Cleveland and Boston, there had been instituted courses on 'Adjustments to Later Maturity and Old Age'.

When Miss Ramsey had been appointed secretary, there were eight regional or county and eighty local Old People's Welfare Committees. When she retired, besides the rapid increase, mentioned earlier, of local committees to reach the number of 831, there were twelve regional and fifty county committees.

In contrast to the painful eking out of petty cash in the first years, for the year ending March 31, 1952, almost £17,000 had been spent on the committee's work, of which the Ministry of Health had provided £5,000 and the National Corporation for the Care of Old People, £3,000.

Besides their expansion, there was, by the nineteen-fifties, a marked development in the character of the activities undertaken or encouraged by the committee. Born in an emergency, it had necessarily been preoccupied with the problems arising from it, though, as we have seen, from the very first it was capable of looking ahead. Now, though many of the problems still persisted – some, indeed, are still with us – it was possible to give more attention to ideas which would enrich the lives of old people, where, previously, merely to make their lives tolerable called for sufficient effort. There was fresh thinking in a variety of directions, and such relatively abstract subjects as preparation for retirement appeared on the programme of annual conferences. The first housing schemes for old people which provided some domestic help were established; more and more local committees set up a chiropody service, than which few measures brought so great benefit with such modest outlay. The Ministry, while it would not include chiropody in the NHS, gave these ventures a blessing by stating that it saw no reason why a voluntary body like an OPW Committee which received a grant under the National Assistance Act for the general purposes of the organization should not use the money for chiropody, which was undoubtedly a part of welfare.

Here and there experiments were made in providing temporary hospital care for the frail elderly living in their own homes, so that the relatives or friends who looked after them might themselves have a holiday. Laundry schemes became more general; arrangements for night attendance were encouraged by a statement in the House of Commons that the Ministry was prepared – as far as funds permitted – to deal sympathetically with proposals by local authorities. Some local authorities set up mobile libraries for old people, who were visited at home once a fortnight, with no charge, and with an opportunity to make requests for particular books. Ideas reported from the districts ranged from a home bathing scheme in Manchester and Salford, staffed mainly by former hospital orderlies or SRN's, with members of the St John Ambulance Association and the Red Cross, to bulb growing competitions for the house-bound elderly, who were provided with hyacinth bulbs, bowls of fibre and simple instructions in the autumn and exhibited the results in the spring. The report of the Committee on Accidents in the Home, set up in 1947, showed that, in the two years, 1947–9, 60,000 people died from accidents at home compared with 48,000 from accidents on the road, and half the 60,000 were over sixty-five. The realization that many of the accidents to the old were preventable brought an increased attention to the fitting of simple appliances like handles beside baths and handrails on the stairs.

Financially, the possibilities of work for old people were considerably enlarged by the setting up of the King George VI Memorial Foundation. The larger share – two-thirds – of the sum raised, once payment had been made for a statue of the king, went to the development of work for young people. The remaining third, which amounted to £600,000, was devoted to work for the old. Ideas for its use were as diverse as in any field of work which receives a windfall. At one time there was a trend towards sinking large sums into the building of a few 'regardless' clubs for the elderly, which, magnificent as they might have been as exemplars, would have benefited relatively few people.

Finally the money was divided between clubs and training. A capital sum of £40,000, which, within three years, was increased to £105,000, made possible the setting up of the King George VI Social Service Scheme, which provided courses for both voluntary and professional workers with the elderly. A substantial grant went to the WVS – now the WRVS – who used it to establish five new 'all-day' clubs, with permanent premises and facilities of the most comprehensive sort. The scheme also financed a pioneer venture, the club at Camberwell, which was initiated by the NOPWC and the London Council of Social Service. This catered for the infirm and others who, for one reason or another, would be unable to join the more conventional type of club. Its services included transport. There was an ambulance to convey to the club those who would not otherwise have been able to attend. The less severely handicapped were collected from their homes by the club bus. Camberwell, which continues to flourish, was the first of the specially built day centres for the elderly.

The rest of the money was allocated in block grants to the National Old People's Welfare Council, the WVS (this was in addition to the capital sum intended specifically for the 'all-day' clubs), the British Red Cross Society, and the Scotland and Northern Ireland Old People's Welfare Committees. It was intended that the grants should be used to help existing clubs to extend their premises or to improve their equipment and amenities, and to enable new clubs to be established. To that end it was distributed in contributions towards the cost of various projects and admirably fulfilled the intention. Relatively small grants attracted other help and made possible both improvements and new ventures.

Inevitably, those who were involved in the work at almost any level, but particularly at headquarters, were more conscious of the outstanding problems and the enormous amount that needed to be done in almost every department than of what they had achieved. But the achievement was unquestionable, and the tribute of the International Gerontological Congress, mentioned earlier, was deserved. Historically, that congress – for whose social setting the NOPWC provided the secretariat – is likely to be remembered less for any of the discussions it produced than for the public oration of Miss Margery Fry, who was herself then eighty years old.

It was a classic, and recognized as such at the time. Later it was to be published as a pamphlet which continues to sell steadily. In addition, and unlike the generality of classics, it is a practical document for those setting out to provide services for old people which remains valid today. Before going on to examine in more detail the different aspects of the work in which the NOPWC is involved, it is worth quoting at some length from Miss Fry's remarkable declaration of the spirit in which all such work must be attempted if those who were served were to keep their dignity and individuality. She herself saw gerontologists as interpreters, 'interpreters not only of old age to its juniors but also of old age to itself'.

'Like Sir Alexander Fleming with his mould,' she told them, 'you have found right under your noses as it were, an under-explored field of study and a field which is rapidly expanding. We are, rather painfully, aware of the shift towards old age of the population, but quite how marked it is becomes apparent only when we take a fairly long view. . . .

'One result of the scarcity of veterans in the past has still, I think, its effect today. Until recent times, very little of what has been written with regard to our last years has come from first-hand experience. The world's authors have, in the main, described youth from within, old age from without, for the world's authors, with but few exceptions, have been writing in comparative youth. . . . Wonderful observations of old age there have been many – it is a common theme throughout the centuries – but they are as a rule the observations of younger people. . . .

'(but) . . . I believe if anyone would take the trouble to make an anthology of the portraits of ancient men and women in literature, these would fall into far fewer types than those in a similar anthology of, let us say, young lovers. I do not know whether this tendency in literature towards standardizing old age in a few types is in part the cause, or wholly a symptom, of a common habit of classification of old people by their age. Nobody expects all middle-aged men to be alike; no one really likes to be regarded as only one of a set. Neither dons nor dust-men wish to be assumed to be purely typical of their profession or occupation. To an administrator an old woman may be just "that old woman, I think her name is Jones" but to herself she is *the* Katie Jones who won a prize for scripture and had the smallest waist in her class – with a thousand other distinctive features – who just happens to be old.

'The specific quality seen from outside is a mere accident felt from within, no more a personal characteristic than an illness might be; in fact I believe to many old people their age hardly seems to belong to them at all. This may seem far-fetched, but

I have checked it in talking to a good many of my contemporaries, and I think it has a real bearing on the interpretation of one generation to another, which I hope you regard as one of your main functions.'

It is not to exaggerate to see that task as the very *raison d'être* of a body like the NOPWC in the latter half of the twentieth century. Material problems there will always be, and however remarkable our advances in comfort and physical well-being, it is safe to say that old people will always be a little behind in feeling the benefit of them. But all the same, as the general standard of living rises, what is today regarded as outstanding, if not luxurious provision in the way of homes and clubs for them will become the norm. A realization of their individuality can by no means be taken for granted in the same way. It is particularly imperilled by the fact that, in our age, the new Greeks are the Americans, who share the Hellenic worship of the youthful body while showing no very great tendency to share the Hellenic veneration for the sage and making every effort to ignore or avoid the fact of death. It is not the easiest climate in which to be old.

Miss Fry, having posed the problem, went on, not so much to give advice as to make clear what old people themselves wanted before all else.

'I suppose,' she said, 'one of the main difficulties of planning for the care of the aged is just this: to respect their personalities whilst grouping their infirmities. The miseries of a life-long democratic intellectual person condemned to a perpetual conversation about the minor doing of the fashionable and great, and perhaps a few of the doings of the cat or dog thrown in, may counterbalance much thoughtful provision for physical comfort. It is more important, where groups are to be formed, to consider tastes than income.

'As the limits of self-determination grow narrower, the ageing person clings more anxiously to what remains. Young people who have outgrown a stormy childhood will tell you that the rock on which their good behaviour came to shipwreck was constantly the irritation at having decisions about themselves made over their heads. To the old, too, choice is a precious prerogative.

'In the world of prison, where every detail is dictated by

discipline, the earning of even a few pence, giving a minute option between cigarettes and sweets, is found to bring relief to tension. And so the old man who can no longer decide between Blackpool and Bournemouth, or between Switzerland and Swaziland for a holiday, whose world has shrunk to the dimensions of a child's, needs above all things to have every possible remnant of self-expression preserved. "Everything needful provided" seems the death-knell of his individual being.

'It is this sensitive claim to retain one's personality even when physical self-determination is limited which makes it so essential in homes for old people, to allow for single rooms—even the smallest slip of a room—where a few of those possessions which are, as it were, almost an extension of themselves, can be housed and where they can fully be themselves. In a sense our intimate possessions are part of ourselves. For the old our false teeth and spectacles are very nearly parts of our body, and things which we continually use and handle are impregnated with our personality. This is specially true of those whose possessions are few. To take them away from an old person is to diminish his very being. He must have somewhere, as we say, "to himself". By many people who have not been over particular in their way of life, a prison with its separate cells is openly admitted to be preferable to an institution with public wards.

'I have spoken of the need for those who make a study of the latter end of life to re-interpret with insistence the old to their successors. There is no one point upon which I feel stress needs to be more constantly laid than this, that the external stigmata of old age must not be allowed to obscure the lasting divergencies of character; individuality must be respected.'

The last, important as it is for all, and increasingly difficult as it is to ensure at all times when there is public provision of many needs which, formerly, were met—in so far as they were met—on a more personal level, is vital for the old, who, as Miss Fry so poignantly described, have seen more and more of what made up their lives stripped away from them. In so far as the varied services for the old to which the rest of this book will be devoted lose sight of it, they lose virtue.

CHAPTER VII

The Purpose of Local
Committees

What are local Old People's Welfare Committees for? Such a
question could hardly have been asked at the time when
Circular 11/50, which brought up a crop of them, thick as May
buttercups, was published by the Ministry of Health. Those
who framed it had no more doubt than those who acted upon it
of the function and purpose of such committees. On one level
the Government, which had passed the legislation setting up
the Welfare State, was genuinely anxious that, in doing so, it
should not quench the spirit of voluntary work and self help
which were established features of British social tradition. On
the other it had made legally available a number of services
which it had neither the premises, nor the money, nor the manpower to provide on the scale on which, it soon became evident,
they would be needed. In 1947, for example, only about 7 per
cent of those old people who wished to find vacancies in small
homes were able to do so. This inadequacy of resources was, of
course, in no way unusual. The moment is never opportune for
social reforms, whether they take the form of raising the school-
leaving age, or forbidding women to do the work of pit ponies,
or relieving student nurses of the more pointless kind of
drudgery. The reforms are made notwithstanding, and after
more or less long travail the benefits are felt. In this instance
the Government was aware both that the voluntary societies
which, for generations, had carried on welfare and charitable
work possessed a valuable store of experience and professional
competence and that, without their help, the deficiencies of the
statutory services would be even more glaring. The visiting of
lonely old people, for example, would at that time scarcely even
have been attempted by officers of the local authorities. Before
1948 small homes for old people were virtually the preserve of

73

the voluntary societies. After that year every house acquired and adapted by a voluntary society or a local committee – the era of purpose-built homes was still in the future – was a contribution towards dealing with a desperate situation. While there was never any suggestion that these should be the limit of their activities, in the early years it seems clear that the government looked to the local committees and their constituent voluntary organizations, chiefly for the provision of small homes and the organizing of visiting schemes and clubs for old people.

The NOPWC, which, as early as February, 1946, had published a model constitution for a local Old People's Welfare Committee, was more detailed and comprehensive in its conception of the part which such committees might play. The constitution specified that fact-finding and education and publicity in fields related to its object were part of such a committee's work, but the crucial clauses were the two first. As set out in 'Old People's Welfare', the original handbook of the NOPWC, these stated that the objects for which an Old People's Welfare Committee was founded were:

(1) To promote and assist the general good of all old people in the area covered by assisting the work of statutory authorities and voluntary organizations engaged in providing facilities for physical and mental recreation, developing physical improvement, furthering health, relieving poverty, distress or sickness or in pursuing any objects which now are or hereafter may be deemed by law to be charitable. (This charitable form of constitution ensured exemption from Income Tax, besides favourable conditions for the payment of certain other duties. It was later amended to meet a new situation in the charity law.)

(2) To promote and organize co-operation in the achievement of the above purposes and to that end to bring together in Council representatives of the authorities and organizations engaged in the furtherance of the above purposes or any of them within the area.

From the beginning it was made clear that, while the bounds of work for old people were wide indeed, the primary function of a local committee was less to take action itself than to co-ordinate action already being taken by existing bodies and to make action possible by inducing co-operation between different agencies. This was emphasized in the clause on membership in the original constitution, whose principle has been preserved in later versions. It was laid down that membership should have the representational character of that of the National Council, with a proviso that no organization should have no more than two representatives. The Committee might 'appoint a Secretary and such other officers and staff as may from time to time be deemed necessary to act for such period, and may pay such remuneration as they think fit'. This last was of vital importance, though it is doubtful if it was always recognized as such at the time. Side by side with the statement of principle went a note on finance: 'The Committee may accept, borrow and raise money for the purpose of the Committee's objects by means of grants in aid from central or local government authorities, donations and legacies, subscriptions from individual members or persons and other sources.'

Nothing in all this, of course, precluded a local committee's taking action itself if it was the only, or even the obvious body to do so and, indeed, local committees had already showed much initiative. Plymouth had established a domestic help scheme. Since December, 1944, local authorities had been empowered to extend their Home Help Schemes to cover the sick and infirm, whether from old age or other causes, but in practice many of them were obliged still to confine them to mothers with young children (for which the service had originally been established) because of the difficulty of finding recruits. Occasionally a voluntary body was better placed to enrol people who would not normally have offered themselves for domestic service but were interested in the idea of helping old people. This was so in Plymouth, where the Assistance Board met the cost – where, that is, the old person needing help was receiving public assistance – and the local committee recruited the workers. By August, 1947, they had thirty-six Home Helps, some working full time, some for only a few hours each week, who, between them, were helping about 150 old people.

In advertising for them the local committee had stressed the fact that the work was a form of service to one's fellows, rather than just another job, and they were successful in attracting older housewives and other responsible middle-aged women. The social service aspect of the work was emphasized by the fact that the secretary of the committee had a weekly meeting and discussion with the helps, and by weekly visits to the old people by volunteers who collected the fees. Both the visitor and the secretary kept records – quite clearly this was visualized from the first as more than the conventional Home Help service. At Woolwich, in an area which had a large elderly population, the local committee had been instrumental in running a lunch club. The London County Council, as it then was, provided through the agency of the Londoners' Meals' Service, a one course meal for which they charged sixpence, the condition being that the Old People's Welfare Committee found a room, served the meals and did the washing up. A rota of thirty volunteers provided the necessary service, the members coming from the WVS, the Co-operative Women's Guilds and the churches, and soon the club had more than 200 customers, aged sixty-five or more, of whom fifty or sixty turned up each day for lunch – soon extended to 'afters' and a cup of tea to follow – and, almost as eagerly, for the company they found there. In Chelsea a mobile canteen service had been operating since December 1945 to provide hot meals for the housebound and infirm elderly. Here the Red Cross and the WVS ran the service and the Old People's Welfare Committee met the cost of maintaining the mobile units. Here, again, the Londoners' Meals' Service provided the lunches, and candidates for them were recommended by district nurses, doctors, the Family Welfare Association and the local Welfare Visitors of the Assistance Board.

The three services quoted were typical rather than being isolated efforts. They have been described in some detail because their organization illustrates particularly well the essential function of a local committee, which is to mobilize and co-ordinate all the available services, working with the statutory authorities as partners rather than setting up rival schemes.

Later years were to bring a proliferation of activities which sprang up to meet new needs as they arose or were discovered. It is hard indeed to think of any service or amenity for the old which is not being provided through one or more of the 1,558 local Old People's Welfare Committees which were operating in the United Kingdom in 1967. Clubs and meals and homes continue though, nowadays, voluntary organizations seldom feel that opening new homes, unless it might be for certain categories of the elderly whom it is difficult to accommodate elsewhere, is a wise policy. To them have been added schemes for holidays, particularly for the housebound, schemes for employment, provision for laundry and hairdressing, housing and schemes for boarding out the elderly. Once every three years the National Council makes a survey of the services for the elderly which are being provided by voluntary organizations, collecting the information by circulating questionnaires to local committees. The answers received have more than statistical interest. They are a contribution to the body of knowledge on which effective administration must be based, and strictures about the value of the answers provided by 'unsophisticated housewives filling in forms on their kitchen tables' have no serious validity. But the question rests and has gained a corollary. What are local Old People's Welfare Committees for and to what extent are they carrying out their function?

The answer to the first question is implicit in the constitution. Local committees exist to do, or help to do, or cause to be done, anything which will further the well-being of old people. Before all else it is their job to discover the existing situation and the available resources in their area – that is, how many people of pensionable age it contains, how many voluntary bodies are active in it and what services they are providing, and what help is available from other sources, State, local authority, or, in some instances, long established local charities. Next they must bring together these agencies, so as to avoid overlapping and make possible schemes which no one of them could establish alone. Pre-eminently this means bringing about in the statutory and voluntary bodies a mutual recognition of what the other can offer.

In the early stages this was not always an easy task. The attitudes of the 'amateurs' and the 'professionals' towards each other varied from mutual incomprehension to equally mutual bristling hostility. In retrospect the picture seems absurd, but those who were in any way involved in voluntary work during the nineteen-forties will remember the profound trauma which the coming of the Welfare State produced in many of their co-workers. All they had laboured for, they were convinced, was to be laid waste and turned over to bumbling bureaucrats who were 'only in it for the money'. The statutory workers, for their part, harboured a composite image of patronizing gentlewomen who sat on committees in forbidding hats, knowing little of how the majority of people lived and nothing of the details of welfare work. The fact that they themselves seldom possessed a social work qualification served, of course, to intensify rather than eradicate this defensive superiority. Since, twenty years ago, Britain had hardly started on the road towards the classless society, the whole was often complicated by the intricacies of the caste system. That, from the very beginning, there were instances of both sides working together with understanding, and with benefit to each other as well as to those they were seeking to serve, was almost always due to the good will and good sense of individuals rather than to a wholesale change in the climate of opinion, and it would have been surprising indeed if it had been otherwise.

What is disquieting is that today, twenty years on, traces of the old attitudes linger, and there are areas where there is no real consultation between local committees and the statutory authorities. What is one to think, for instance, of a county committee which, when faced with a Ministry of Health circular sent out to urge once more the need for co-operation between OPW Committees and local authorities if the ten-year hospital health and welfare plans were to be more than a series of pious hopes, decided that to meet their particular local authority would be 'a waste of time'? It is possible that their earlier experiences had been unfortunate.

Nevertheless, when one reads in the notes of the same meeting of secretaries of another county committee which did arrange to see County Council representatives, and, in consequence, had its grant raised from £200 a year to £2,500 a year, which made possible for the first time the appointment of a full-time paid officer, it is hard to escape the idea that more enterprise on the part of the first committee might have turned out to be profitable. There is, in fact, a growing body of evidence to suggest that the prejudice of statutory authorities against voluntary bodies as such is greatly diminished, though it may not have disappeared. But, particularly in our recurrent periods of financial restriction, local authorities, from county councils downwards, who make grants must be certain that the money they are disbursing will be efficiently employed. In so far as a local Old People's Welfare Committee presents an image of fumbling benevolence, it will neither get nor deserve to get grants.

Where, however unjustly, that is the image which does prevail, the root cause, in the vast majority of cases, is not the quality of the practical work inspired or carried out by the committee in question, but administrative weaknesses. These, in their turn, are most often due to lack of funds. To quote the 1962 annual report of the National Old People's Welfare Council:

'Most old people's welfare committees work on shoestring budgets, without proper offices, and depending on the devoted services of part-time voluntary secretaries. Many of these committees can do only a proportion of what they would wish to do. It has been found again and again that a committee with a paid secretary and an office readily accessible can mobilize, train and successfully deploy enough voluntary helpers to provide the services needed.'

The difficulty here is that administration is not an appealing object for fund-raising. It is relatively easy to gain public sympathy for a scheme for setting up a luncheon club for old people, or for giving them a Christmas party, or for opening a day centre, but very difficult indeed to catch the imagination and attract the contributions of the public with a call for funds with which to pay a secretary. This is understandable enough: office management is not a subject to which the average layman kindles naturally. What is more unfortunate is that there are local authorities which seem to share that attitude. There have been instances of authorities which were ready to support those wishing to take the National Council's training course for matrons of old people's homes, but a good deal less ready to make grants for administrative expenses. Also, there are wide variations in the amounts of grants made by different local authorities to county Old People's Welfare Committees whose needs were roughly comparable. This may be an unconscious legacy from the days when it was believed that money should not be spoken of in connection with good works which were 'all voluntary'. But even a voluntary secretary whose office is her sitting-room or the spare bedroom needs a typewriter and a couple of filing cabinets if she is to do her job efficiently, and the costs of stationery and postage and printing, besides normal out of pocket expenses for necessary travelling for example, mount alarmingly. The need was realized by the National Corporation for the Care of Old People, which, in 1962, set aside a sum of £10,000 for a period of five years to help with staff and administrative costs of old people's welfare committees in certain selected areas. One of the objects of that grant was to show by practical example what the committees could achieve if they were provided with offices and staffs. Only when a secretary has decent working conditions and help to relieve her of such mechanical tasks as typing and duplicating can she devote her energies to her proper task, of which advising her committee on policy, making known its work and helping to sponsor new local committees (this for a regional or county secretary) and support the existing ones makes up an important part. Also, it is unrealistic to expect to be able to attract and keep a suitably qualified and competent secretary, when the post is a paid one, unless her salary corresponds with others of similar responsibility in the field of social work.

Normally those authorities which make grants for administrative costs do so under Section 136 of the Local Government Act 1948, which permits such aid to 'bodies giving advice, information or other assistance' or working 'for the benefit of the area or its residents'. In 1959 a circular (33/59) from the Ministry of Housing and Local Government placed 'entirely within the discretion of local authorities' whether and to what extent they should support certain kinds of voluntary bodies and made specific mention of 'the administrative expenses of Old People's Welfare Committees'. A circular (18/64) issued by the Ministry of Health in 1964 drew the attention of local authorities to this general consent, and hoped they would 'make full use of their powers to contribute to voluntary organizations whose activities further the development of the health and welfare service'. The Amendment Act 1962 of the National Assistance Act, 1948 considerably extended the previous powers of local authorities to help voluntary organizations 'to provide meals and recreation for old people'. And another Ministry of Health circular (18/64) issued in 1964 reminded local authorities of the wide powers they possessed under the National Health Service Act, 1946 and the National Assistance Act, 1948 'to contribute to voluntary organizations which are providing health and welfare services'. Here again there was specific mention of 'financial contributions to voluntary organisations whose activities consist in or include the provision of meals or recreation for old people'.

The Health Service and Public Health Act, 1968, is largely an amending Act, but contains some new matter. In particular, its broad concept of what constitutes welfare gives it importance for the future of work for the elderly. At the time of writing, no date has been given for the putting into operation of two of its most useful sections. Section 13 places on local authorities the duty to provide 'on such a scale as is adequate for the needs of their area' home helps and a laundry service for the sick, aged and handicapped and to charge for them where it sees fit. Section 45 gives very wide cover for a local authority, with the approval of the Minister of Health and to such extent as he may direct, 'to make arrangements for promoting the welfare of old people'. It is specifically stated that the arrangements may cover employing as their agent 'any voluntary organization having for its sole or principal object the promotion of the welfare of old people'. Section 64, which enables the Minister to give assistance by grant or loan to a voluntary organization which 'provides, promotes or publicises' certain services, including accommodation for the elderly and infirm, and arrangements for promoting the welfare of the old may not be implemented 'in the present financial circumstances'.

There is no lack of the necessary powers and there is no doubt that the Government wishes them to be used. The debates in the House of Commons on the 1968 Act provided fresh evidence of the Government's intention to encourage voluntary associations. It might be that a more positive approach by committees to their local authorities would prove effective. Evidence from Birmingham, heard at a meeting of secretaries held in 1965, gives reason to believe this. In that city, voluntary bodies which were receiving very substantial grants had made clear to the local authority that, unless they got such help, they could not pay the salaries which would enable them to employ the staff which the authority itself required.

One consideration which sometimes deters local authorities from applying for grants, or at least from importuning for sufficiently large grants, is the idea that local authority finance will mean local authority control. It is unfounded – unless the perfectly proper wish of any local authority to be assured that an organization to which it gives financial support is efficient and properly run is regarded as 'control'. Independence, however, is important for local committees. Most of those now in existence are both independent and autonomous – that is, they have adopted the model constitution and have an independent secretariat, whether paid or voluntary. Others are independent but not autonomous because their secretary may be attached to another body, such as a Council of Social Service, or may be a local government officer. In addition to these there are a few Old People's Welfare Committees which do not have final responsibility for their own work, or even for their own staff, since they are in fact sub-committees of a Rural Community Council or a Council of Social Service. Lastly, some local authorities have set up and staffed Old People's Welfare Committees which, though they may have some outside members, are in no sense independent bodies.

To stress the importance of independence is not to imply any criticism of the work done for old people by local authorities. It is, rather, to suggest that monopolies are undesirable, whether by statutory or voluntary agencies. Local authorities need the stimulus, the inspiration, sometimes the criticism of a voluntary body engaged in the same work. For an officer of a local authority who is a member of a Local Old People's Welfare Committee it can be a refreshing as well as an instructive experience to see occasionally from another standpoint problems with which he is concerned for a good part of his normal working day. For a member of a voluntary organization it can be an equally helpful one to be a co-opted member of an appropriate local authority committee. The present tendency to bring more and more branches of social work under a single department, and the possibility of still more centralization in future makes even more necessary and valuable the existence alongside the unified statutory service of an independent body wholly concerned with promoting the well-being of the old.

It is possible that Old People's Welfare Committees will shortly be re-named. 'Welfare' has a rather equivocal connotation; many of those over sixty or over sixty-five would repudiate the description 'old'; 'Committee' suggests a subsidiary rather than an autonomous body. Whatever they may be called, in so far as they are fulfilling their function, it will remain true that 'An old people's welfare committee is not just another organization – it is the key organization which brings together in its area all those who are concerned with the care of the elderly. The committee fulfils an urgent need because many different statutory and voluntary agencies have a duty, or concern, or opportunity to help the elderly.'

CHAPTER VIII

Training

'We would do well to temper the over-sentimental approach to the care of the elderly by policies based on common sense and experience. It is little realized in the corridors of power how exacting is the day to day care of residents, or how demanding, ungrateful, and downright rude some old folk can be.

'In this overcrowded island it is ludicrous to imagine that we can continue to cope with the massive growth in the demand for residential accommodation for the elderly with a limited labour force, entirely in small homes. A smaller number of larger homes would be likely to make better use of scarce, competent staff.'

The above quotation (taken from the *Guardian*) is an extract from the discussion at the 1967 conference of the Association of Hospital and Welfare Administrators; the speaker was the superintendent of an old people's home. The questions it raises would provide material for another conference. An edifying exercise might be to substitute 'railway travellers', or 'hotel guests', or 'clients', or 'customers' for the words 'elderly', 'residents' and 'old folk' in the first paragraph and then see how it would read. It may be worth noting in passing that the word 'patients' could be substituted for them without creating much stir, which in itself tells us a good deal of the attitudes which need to be guarded against when an individual or an agency is in the position of providing a service to those who, if only temporarily, are at a disadvantage. At present we will treat it simply as a refutation of the idea, which even today, has some currency, that all one needs for work with old people is common sense and a kind heart.

On his own testimony, the superintendent valued and, no doubt, possessed common sense. There is no reason to think that he did not possess a normally kind heart. What he manifestly lacked was the ability to examine critically certain inherited ideas, and the empathy which would have helped him to realize the cause of much of the 'demandingness', the 'ingratitude' and the 'rudeness' which troubled him. Admittedly, without a kind heart, the best of training cannot produce the right sort of worker, but, assuming its existence, recruits can be helped to gain an understanding of the old which will make their own task more rewarding as well as making the life of their charges more agreeable. In addition they will, of course, need an impressive body of practical knowledge and skill. It is the inculcation and development of the two, side by side, which is the aim of all schemes for training those who work with old people, at whatever level.

From its early days the NOPWC had foreseen that, as more and more voluntary organizations opened small homes for old people, in addition to those which were provided by local authorities, there would be a growing demand for trained staff, and since these new, small homes were setting a pattern, it was important that those who staffed them should be trained in the right way. To anticipate, it was the NOPWC, specifically, a speaker at one of its annual conferences, which pointed the need to set up a national committee to examine the situation in old people's homes. Other bodies later joined the council in bringing pressure on the Government. The committee was finally set up by the National Council of Social Service, financed and grant aided by the Gulbenkian Foundation. With Lady Williams, Professor of Economics, London University, in the chair, it devoted four years to research into the position in both old people's and children's homes. One of the facts revealed in its report, 'Caring for People', published in 1967, was that, at this time, more than 80 per cent of the staff in old people's homes had had no formal training. Also, the turnover of staff in residential homes was about 25 per cent each year.

Later still the NCSS was to join with the National Institute for Social Work Training in setting up a committee to enquire into the rôle of voluntary workers in the social services. The terms of reference of this committee, which was due to report in 1968 or 69, were 'to enquire into the rôle of voluntary workers in the social services. The Committee will consider particularly how the work of the volunteer fits into the total structure of the personal social services; whether there are new settings where they might help; their relationship to professional workers; questions of recruitment and the different contributions of particular age groups; and any preliminary or continuing need for preparation and guidance'. The NOPWC submitted evidence to it, including evidence to the sub-committee which was dealing with aspects of training and its chairman, Mrs Newman, became a member of this sub-committee.

All this was far in the future when, after consultation with the Ministries of Health and Education, the NOPWC, with the aid of a grant from the National Corporation for the Care of Old People, arranged two courses, the first starting in September, 1950, the second in October of the following year. There were more than 150 applications for these two courses, and fifty-four were accepted; thirty candidates for the first and twenty-four for the second. Their ages ranged from twenty-five to fifty, and the numbers applying meant that selection could be rigorous. The successful candidates included trained nurses, women who had been in charge of homes of other types or who had worked in the Welfare Departments of local authorities, and those who had looked after their own aged parents or other relatives. Posts were waiting for them. The second course ended in February, 1952; by the end of March, twenty-one of the twenty-four students who had completed it had found jobs and the National Council was arranging a third course, to begin in the autumn.

Looking back, and comparing these pioneer courses with the present fourteen-and-a-half weeks' training course for the matrons and deputy matrons of homes, it is noticeable that the first lasted six months, the second four. It should not be thought that six months, still less four, was found longer than was necessary to cover a comprehensive syllabus. Sweden, a pioneer in work for the elderly as in other kinds of social work, gave, and still gives, its workers a three-year training. The Williams Committee, when it reported, was to recommend a two-year course, also the establishment of a national training body to foster education and research. The NOPWC itself had first considered a ten months' course. Six months was decided on after discussion with local authorities and others concerned; the later curtailments were dictated by practical expediency rather than principle. The present syllabus for courses starts with three weeks' practical training in a home under an experienced matron, followed by four weeks' theoretic training, and goes on to four weeks' training in a home and a final two days' tuition at a residential centre. The theoretic side covers social history and social legislation, catering, nutrition and food hygiene, office and household management, staff relationships, home nursing, First Aid and the prevention of accidents.

Another factor which has governed the length of the courses is the staff shortage which has become progressively more acute as more and more small homes have been opened, so that, today, any woman who seems reasonably sensible and capable and has some kind of relevant experience, even if it is only domestic, can get and keep a post as an assistant matron without any training at all. Training, in any event, does not bring a salary increase, nor can so short a period lead to a recognized professional qualification. The consequences are inevitable, and figures for recent courses illustrate them startlingly. Nowadays, more than half the students at any given course for the wardens and matrons of homes have been seconded for training by their employers – in itself a testimony to the admitted value of the scheme – who are usually local authorities. The lesser half is drawn from those, whether new to the work or already possessing some experience, who have applied independently.

For the course which started in October, 1965, there were 176 inquiries. They produced forty-five applications, from which twelve students were finally selected to attend the course. In March, 1966, there were 246 inquiries from non-seconded students, or prospective students. The number of firm applications was fourteen, from which four were selected. It is clear that, while present conditions persist, the training courses, through no deficiency of their own, are likely to cater more for those already working in the service than for new recruits.

Their maximum output, if so mechanical a phrase may be permitted, of newly trained candidates for posts as superintendents, matrons or assistant matrons of homes is under forty. Bearing in mind that there are in Britain between 3,500 and 4,000 homes, statutory, voluntary and private (the figure given by Peter Townsend in his survey *The Last Refuge*, published in 1962, was 3,644) it is simply derisory. It is worth remembering, also, that the NOPWC is, at the time of writing, the only agency providing formal training and that nothing in our present economic position gives ground for hoping that the recommendations of the Williams Committee on Staffing of Residential Homes and Institutions will soon be put into effect.

From early days, the National Council has realized the needs of those who are already holding positions in homes. Its first refresher course for superintendents, matrons or assistants was provided in 1949; at present about ninety students a year benefit from them. Each course lasts from five to seven days, and the tendency is to build up each around some particular aspect of the work. Subjects dealt with over the years mirror both the changing nature of problems in homes and changes in our ideas of what should be the priorities in the task of looking after the old. Of late such matters as the care of the infirm and personal relationships within homes have taken precedence over, say, catering and nutrition or statutory provisions. It would be hard to exaggerate the value of these courses, both in keeping staff in touch with the progress of ideas, and with newly-won understanding of the old and their problems, and in promoting discussion and intellectual cross-fertilization among women–who remain the vast majority, though there is a sprinkling of men on the courses–who are in essentially lonely positions. If they did nothing but restore perspective, by making a harassed matron realize that her problems are common to many, they would justify their existence. For those who are appointed to their posts on the basis of experience and/or aptitude only, which means the great mass of those now employed as the superintendents or matrons of homes, these 'refreshers' represent all the formal training they are likely to get.

Part of the grant which the NOPWC received from the King George VI Foundation–within three years it was increased from the original £40,000 to £105,000–has gone towards supporting these 'professional' courses. When, in 1955, the ten years' term of the scheme as it was originally conceived came to an end, the National Corporation for the Care of Old People once more stepped in to ensure that they should continue until 1968. By then it was hoped that the findings of the Williams Committee would have led to the establishment of a national training scheme for the staff of homes–a hope which was born before the 'squeeze'. Mainly, however, the King George VI Foundation grant was earmarked for the training of voluntary workers. The concept was novel, if not revolutionary. Previously, in the mind of authority, as well as of the public, voluntary workers had been by definition both untrained and unskilled, supplying in good will what they lacked in expertise and busying themselves with 'do-goodery' chiefly to satisfy their upward urges. The fact that the existing body of knowledge of the principles of social work has been based on the experience of the pioneers of the nineteenth century, most of whom were purely amateurs, was not likely to shake that kind of accepted opinion. Now, with the demand for welfare services suddenly growing far beyond the capacity of the local authorities to meet it, there came a realization that voluntary effort was the only possible source of extra pairs of hands, and that it would be as well if they were not too butter-fingered.

The NOPWC's plan was for systematic short-term training, aimed at the different categories of helpers who were involved in working for old people. For key workers – secretaries or other officers of Old People's Welfare Committees, organizers of the more ambitious clubs which were open all day for five or six days a week, organizers of voluntary visiting schemes and those who might act as tutors for local training, there were residential courses, organized nationally, lasting from five to seven days. Regionally, there were training schemes, under a recognized tutor, for those able and willing to organize local courses. These local courses, consisting of a minimum of six hours of training sessions, often spread out over several weeks, were intended for the average voluntary helper in a number of fields. Club workers, those who delivered Meals on Wheels, voluntary visitors, might be brought together on the same course. At their appropriate levels of detail and profundity these three types of course covered a comprehensive field, ranging from attitudes towards age and towards aged people to occupational interests, from the prevention of accidents in the home to the work of old people's welfare committees. Besides these general courses, there were specialized ones for individual groups, such as club leaders, voluntary visitors, volunteer handicraft teachers, which concentrated on the particular aspects with which they would deal. By April 1966, more than 21,000 voluntary or paid workers, of whom the voluntary made up by far the larger proportion, had taken part in this training.

Results are not of the kind that can be assessed tangibly – it is obviously impracticable to mount an experiment in which the same group of voluntary workers could be compared carrying out the same tasks before and after training. The most convincing evidence that this is a worth while enterprise, and recognized as such, is the growing number of statutory authorities who are now making grants towards local training courses. In some areas, indeed, where the local OPW has not begun to train its voluntary workers, the statutory authorities are prodding them into action. Elsewhere there is the traditional picture of a statutory authority's having taken over a scheme first tried out by a voluntary body. In London boroughs, evening institutes and institutes for further education are now including local courses in their syllabus. The courses for full-time workers which were originally provided by the London and Middlesex Old People's Welfare Committee have been taken over by the education authority, and a Polytechnic now arranges one or two each year. Kent offers an example of a development in training which, when it was instituted, was unique in this country, though it must be hoped that it will not long remain so. There the local education authority makes an annual grant to the County Old People's Welfare Committee, which enables an organizing tutor to work permanently in the county. It has also helped with training courses, sometimes indirectly by providing premises and paying for special tutors. This has meant that, besides an active programme of training for workers engaged in general work among the elderly, it has been possible to establish refresher courses for matrons of residential homes for old people. Probably this is the pattern of assistance which the NOPWC would most welcome. Another interesting scheme has been tried in Cumberland, where the Council of Social Service and the Old People's Welfare Committee have set up a joint training committee, on which both the extra-mural department of Newcastle University and the Workers' Educational Association are represented.

Obviously, when legislation is liable to change, the welfare provision, if it is to be equal to its task, must be in a constant state of development, voluntary helpers, however simple the tasks they undertake individually, need to have a working knowledge of the kind of help they can call on, even if it is only – perhaps, here, particularly when it is only – about such concrete matters as the possibility of obtaining a special grant for an old lady whose much-used blankets will not see her through another winter, or of having a handrail fitted on a steep staircase which has to be negotiated by an increasingly frail householder.

Also, while it is true that if a prospective voluntary visitor does not possess the qualities of courtesy and friendliness no amount of training is likely to make him or her acceptable to the elderly, or, indeed, to anyone else, some teaching about the nature of old age will enable those who already have a right disposition to give a great deal more pleasure to those upon whom they bestow their company. It might be useful here if the old themselves could take a more active share in training, at least at the local level. There are occasions when one suspects that the majority of those concerned in providing for the old people in their locality are themselves sufficiently elderly to be slightly arthritic, emotionally and mentally, while still not being old enough to have first-hand knowledge of the needs of age, its fears, its frustrations, its contentment, its real and enduring sources of enjoyment and pleasure and its capacity for fun.

In the long view, however, it may be that schemes for training voluntary workers at the local level will prove most valuable for their contribution to altering the climate of public opinion, to inculcating an awareness of the general condition of age as well as of the predicament of certain individuals among the elderly, and to spreading the idea that there are sources of help which can be approached when the need arises. So, for one voluntary visitor who has learned how to be a more welcome and more helpful guest in the homes of her elderly friends, there will be others not directly concerned in old people's welfare who will have been alerted to danger signals in the circumstances of an ageing neighbour who lives alone, or who see the point of starting a housing association for the elderly, or who have been brought to realize the need to make some provision beyond the simply material for their own old age. If, indeed, it proves to be so, it will be a remarkable return on the original investment. Already there are signs that the interest will be forthcoming.

CHAPTER IX

The Years of Retirement

Training to fit oneself for voluntary work with old people may still, for the general public, be a relatively novel concept, but, once they are brought to consider it, the majority of potential recruits are likely to admit that it is a logical one. Training to be an old person, which is what training for retirement must imply, is a different matter. In some the idea arouses an instinctive hostility, born of dread. In others, possibly a larger number, there is what may seem a natural aversion to the artificiality of deliberate preparation for what is a natural and inevitable state of life. Last, over the whole thing there hangs a whiff of the notion of 'taking care of oneself' to an excessive degree which is likely to repel such of the middle-aged as are normally healthy in mind and body. If most people would agree that it is better to be dead than decrepit, there is a sizeable minority which feels that it is better to be dead than 'well-preserved', with all the term implies of denial of life and renunciation of the exhilarating prospect of dropping in one's tracks, at whatever age.

That is the climate in which, long before 1955, when it appointed a study group to consider the question, the NOPWC has been devoting attention to preparation for retirement. During the previous year, the Ministry of Health annual report, a document not normally given to fantasy or excessively impractical ideas, suggested that 'timely planning can do much to anticipate and prevent hardship to the elderly at a later date'. As early as 1949, the NOPWC had devoted a good deal of time at its national conference – the fourth – to consideration of various aspects of the question. True, the formal subject of a session at which Sir Ernest Rock Carling, a Trustee of the Nuffield Provincial Hospitals Trust presided, was the scope and possibilities of employment for old people – itself a matter of considerable importance to the retired – but the content ranged widely.

Close on twenty years later there is still a contemporary ring about the opinions of the speakers, who, besides the chairman, included the late W. A. Sanderson, then Assistant Secretary of the Nuffield Foundation, Mrs Barbara Lewis, later to become Mrs Shenfield, Senior Tutor in Social Studies, University of Birmingham and Mr Richard Clements, Deputy Secretary of the National Council of Social Service. There was general agreement that boredom was one of the scourges of old age, that work, provided it was suitable work, was of great importance to health, particularly for men, that an arbitrary retiring age of sixty or sixty-five had little to commend it and that many a man had been 'killed by retirement'. Women, here, fare better, because they seldom retire from housework. One or two speakers from the floor of the house talked of the constructive use of leisure, apart from possibilities of continuing at work. Clearly the seeds of preparation for retirement were here, though at this time there was no suggestion of setting up a committee to study it. At this conference, incidentally, Sir Geoffrey King, the then Deputy Secretary, Ministry of National Insurance, and later Permanent Secretary to the Ministry of Pensions and National Insurance, said that at that time 60 per cent of people of retirement age were still at work, and it had been estimated that 25 per cent of the self-employed were also continuing to work.

It is a fact that retirement as we know it today is a highly artificial as well as a relatively new phenomenon. We often forget how recent in the life of our civilization is the kind of wage-labour which is governed by the alarm clock and the factory hooter, and whose starting gun is a fifteenth birthday as the tape is a sixtieth or sixty-fifth. In a simpler society, where the family was a productive unit, the young started as soon as they were able and performed such tasks as they could manage while the old did gradually less. It would be wrong to be romantic or sentimental about this system, but, at least, there was no question of being in full production on Friday and on Monday morning being left to stand empty handed and uncomprehending. Nor was there much question of retirement for the wage-earner in the nineteenth century.

Conditions were such that there were not large numbers of the elderly, and those who did reach any age were compelled to go on working as long as they could since the alternative was existence on their own savings, if they had any, eked out by what their children could spare. Retirement as we know it is related to a population of whom the majority may expect to reach old age – it is worth remembering that, sixty years ago, average expectation of life for a man was a little more than forty-eight years, for a woman little more than fifty-two years – and to the existence of a pensions scheme which not only permits but may insist upon retirement at a given age. Even today the self-employed and members of the professions seldom stop in that abrupt fashion. The watchmaker, the cabinet-maker, pursue their absorbing craft until hand and eye tire. The higher Civil Servant may leave Whitehall at sixty, but it is usually to a busy five years of acting as chairman to commissions and assisting investigations of one kind or another. The elderly lawyer decides he will come into the office on four days a week only; the older doctor leaves more of the running round to his juniors while he makes the best use of his perfected skill in less exhausting ways. Business men, unless they are unfortunate enough to have sunk into the manic state of 'living for their work', turn to public affairs. These are various kinds of adjustment, not to traumatic change, but to the organic development of one's life. It is doubly hard that, for those who are, as it were, shocked into idleness, there are certain features of modern life which make the process even more painful. One is the extraordinary rapidity of change, both technological and sociological, which means that while in previous generations the elderly were the transmitters of traditional skills and the repositories of accumulated wisdom, in our own a craftsman who learned his job twenty years ago must be re-orientated and the family is scattered over a decaying city centre, a housing estate or new town miles outside it, and, perhaps, a couple of universities at the other end of the country. Additionally, the demographic pattern of our country since the beginning of the century means that 25 per cent of today's old people are unmarried or childless and so cannot count on children or grandchildren for help or company. There is no need to stress that there are corresponding gains, in which the elderly have shared, even if, usually, they are the last to benefit.

The NOPWC's decision, in 1955, to appoint a Study group to consider the whole question of preparation for retirement and to advise on desirable action to be taken, was a natural consequence of its own continuing interest in a subject which, though most of the early work on it had been done in the United States, was arousing more and more attention in Britain. In 1952, four British universities, or university colleges, Exeter, Sheffield, Bristol and Hull, following the lead which had been given in the USA, particularly at the universities of Chicago and Michigan, arranged appropriate courses for the elderly or ageing. Perhaps inevitably at this stage they were attended chiefly by people who were working for the elderly. As, with other efforts intended for the public good, it is commonly that section of the public whose need is the least acute which is the first to make use of them, so one of the root problems of preparation for retirement is that courses offered are likely to attract the more competent and enterprising of the aging, who have probably already gone some way in making plans for their own retirement.

Also in 1952 the Ministry of Labour set up its National Advisory Committee on the Employment of Older Men and Women, which was later to publish two reports. The subject had previously been considered by the National Joint Advisory Council, representing the British Employers' Confederation, the Trades Union Congress and the nationalized industries, which had recognized the need for making possible the greater employment of older men and women, but the NOPWC very justifiably felt that it could claim credit for stimulating public interest. At its national conference in that same year it devoted a major session to the employment problems of the elderly. The speaker was the Minister of Labour, Sir Walter Monckton, who spoke of the committee he had decided to set up, and in the chair was Arthur Deakin, then Chairman of the TUC and General Secretary of the Transport and General Workers' Union.

The Study Group, whose membership constituted an impressive body of experience and expertise, met twenty-three times between February 1955 and February 1959, during which time it became unmistakably clear that there was a permanent need for such a body. The Preparation for Retirement Committee was accordingly set up and a grant from the National Corporation for the Care of Old People made possible the appointment of an officer to carry out the recommendations of the study group over the next three years. For several years the committee acted as a clearing house for ideas and information on every aspect of preparing for retirement. In 1963 its connection with the NOPWC was severed – though mutual interest and co-operation remained – because it was felt there was good psychological reasons for removing the subject from the context of work for old people. Already study and observation had shown that if preparation for retirement was to be useful it must be started in middle life, and the middle-aged were likely to be deterred by association with an organization devoted to the welfare of the elderly. For a while the committee was linked with the National Council of Social Service. Early in 1964 it adopted its own constitution and was established under the name of the Pre-Retirement Association as a legal charity with a mission rather akin, in its own field, to that of the NOPWC among local old people's committees, in that an important part of its work consisted of stimulating local efforts and encouraging collaboration in every way.

Meanwhile there had been increasing evidence of national interest in the subject at a variety of levels, from research into the learning capacities of the elderly who were trained for new jobs to setting up of local committees in many parts of the country. In 1958 Glasgow set up a Retirement Council which brought together representatives of the Corporation, the University, the Glasgow Trades Council and the British Institute of Management, among other bodies. Its aims included providing facilities for handicrafts and hobbies for those already retired, as well as providing education for retirement, and here, too, a grant from the National Corporation for the Care of Old People permitted the appointment of a full-time officer to work in the city. Elsewhere more and more organizations ran their own courses, often stimulated and guided by the national committee.

Once their interest is captured, and their initial resistance overcome, the majority of people acknowledge the value of such help. When, in the autumn of 1958, the NOPWC, through the generosity of the Calouste Gulbenkian Foundation, was able to arrange a pioneer study week-end during which people from a broad spectrum of society were brought together to consider how they would spend the latter part of their lives, the general manager of an insurance company, a coalminer, a saleswoman, a doctor, a bank manager, a local government officer, a housewife, a bus driver, a confectioner, a trade unionist and a nursing sister were all ready to admit that 'there's something in it for me'. On the practical side, indeed, even the most forward-looking are likely to benefit from a comprehensive information service, which may begin with an outline of the chances of finding part-time work if this attracts them. When, a few years ago, the Over Forty Association for Women decided to investigate the possibilities of finding work for women over sixty, it discovered that many of them did not know that, even if they had accepted a pension at sixty instead of waiting until they were sixty-five, they could still register with the Ministry of Labour for employment if this seemed likely to be useful. Nor did they know that the much resented Earnings Rule, which limits the amount which a pensioner can earn before the pension is reduced proportionately, allows him or her to earn that sum clear of expenses like fares, Income Tax and insurance, which, for a person living on the outskirts of London or any other large town, and travelling in to work daily, is no trifle. The whole question of part-time work, like that of compulsory retiring ages, is, of course, dominated by the current situation in the labour market. From an employment situation in which employers may have been eager to encourage at least certain skilled workmen to continue after the age of sixty-five, we may be moving into a period when new industrial techniques, quite apart from intermittent patches of unemployment, may dictate, besides a shorter working week, a far lower age for compulsory retirement.

Contrary to widely held beliefs, automation is unlikely to bring better prospects for the older worker. It may provide what are traditionally known as 'light' jobs, but they are usually jobs which call for a fairly high degree of speed and co-ordination, both of which are more taxing to the elderly than tasks requiring more physical effort. For some workers the present retiring age is even higher than sixty-five. It must have come as a surprise to many to learn, not so long ago, that dockers, whose job, if any, must certainly rank as heavy work, were contesting a proposal to reduce their compulsory retiring age from sixty-eight to sixty-five. In the kind of future which seems probable, the opportunities for part-time work may turn out to be chiefly among the less orthodox ventures, particularly, perhaps, in the provision of a variety of those 'made to measure' personal services which, in a highly industrialized society, are so hard to obtain.

There is room, too, for a comprehensive and unbiased financial information service whose field would range from persuading the over-independent that extra welfare grants are not 'charity' to setting out the relative merits of annuities, lump sum insurance schemes and putting one's savings into a building society. Many people know little or nothing of the possibilities of development or improvement grants when they are considering adapting their houses; many are vague about the relative costs of various systems of heating them; some, when they consider spending their retirement in another part of the country, may not have considered the level of the local rates when planning their future budget, or, if we are to be mercilessly realistic, have not considered their chances of obtaining a hospital bed at need in an area whose population is topheavy with the elderly and retired. The decision whether to move at all is less simple than is sometimes represented by psychiatrists who suggest that to tear up one's roots past sixty is to invite a lonely and insecure old age. That may be sadly true. But what of those whose jobs have meant that they have had no chance to put down roots, whether they have been Methodist ministers or building site workers? What of the chronic bronchitic who loves the friendly warmth of his native Northern industrial town whose atmosphere is slowly killing him, or the tenant of a London flat whose rent would eat up his pension? Preparation for retirement involves helping people to consider such problems and to work them out for themselves, never, of course, imposing a solution or even commending too strongly any course of action.

With the emotional side of preparation for old age, one is on more difficult ground. It is no less true for being a cliché that a rewarding and fulfilled old age is the crown of a rewarding life, which has had its due share of work and recreation and interests, its friendships and its affectionate family relationships, and preparation for that, for better or worse, must begin in the nursery and continue in the classroom. Middle age is late, perhaps too late, to start, and there is, in any case, something faintly repugnant about the idea of urging a woman of forty to develop an interest in tapestry work or a man of fifty to be rather more patient with the golf club's licensed bore because, by so doing, they will be improving their chances of mental health in old age. Unless undertaken for their own sakes, neither is likely to bear much fruit. It is even more painfully true, as one piece of sociological research after another has shown us, that, for men particularly, in a society as dominated by work as is our own, retirement means not only the loss of the status that goes with income but to some extent loss of identity also; for if one aspect of status is the ability occasionally to stand one's friends a round, a large part of identity depends upon being known among them as a turner, or a welder, or a platelayer, or a plumber or whatever. To become overnight a man without a defined function whose wife likes him out of the house in the mornings calls for considerable powers of adjustment. One valuable asset is to have developed a second identity, as bowls club secretary or church sidesman or local snooker champion. Another is to have an interest like fishing or growing prize chrysanthemums which is more absorbing than what is sometimes implied by the word 'hobby', with its overtones of trifling.

In general, therefore, the aim of the growing number of courses in preparation for retirement which have been set up by various agencies for adult education has been to indicate to those still well below retiring age the possibilities that are open to them when at last they have the leisure to pursue interests which, during their working lives, have had to take a minor place. Perhaps they may be led to use some of the spare time which often comes with later middle age, when children are no longer entirely demanding, to investigate the possibilities of the local evening classes. Men, in particular, often have no idea of what they offer. They are apt to dismiss them as 'all fancy cookery and flower arranging' when in fact a craftsman might find in them an opportunity to exercise for pleasure his skill as a cabinet maker or to develop one new and undreamed of as a silversmith. If further endorsement were needed of the value of such courses, it is to be found in the increasing interest which they are arousing in industry. At the midland engineering works of the firm of Rubery Owen, all workers on the shop floor when they reach the age of fifty are invited to take part in weekly discussion groups which consider the problems of retirement. In the first year of the scheme, only one-third responded. By the third year, half the eligible men applied to join. The course included a residential week-end to which wives were invited–which would seem essential to any useful planning for a joint future. Later the scheme was extended from the shop floor to the staff, a reversal of the more normal procedure, since the Institute of Directors has in general been more alert to the problems, other than financial, of enforced leisure, than have the trade unions. In Glasgow the Retirement Council launched an experimental day release course, in which seven firms co-operated by allowing their employees time off on full pay to attend at the College of Further Education, as they might have done for their apprentices. The average age here was rather higher; the course was aimed at those between fifty-five and sixty-five, and the mean turned out to be around sixty. The lectures covered the economics of retirement, its medical, social and psychological aspects and educational possibilities. The aim was to excite interest. Once it was kindled, it was hoped that the members of the course would go on to cultivate it by way of the education authorities' classes or the extra-mural department of the university. With that in mind, fifty might seem a better age to start than sixty, though it is impossible to be arbitrary about it. Fifty is certainly a better age at which to receive simple health teaching, beginning, perhaps, with the development of a proper spirit of scepticism about the claims of patent medicine manufacturers and going on to some elementary facts about food and its relation to well-being. At that age there is some hope that advice might be followed. To hope to change the habits of a lifetime past the age of sixty is to be optimistic indeed in most cases.

If no mention has been made in all this of the importance of an adequate income on retirement, it is because it has been taken for granted as a first essential. Teaching on how to manage on a reduced income does not involve preaching resignation in poverty, and whatever other activities the NOPWC may venture on in the future, ensuring that pension scales keep pace with the rise in the cost of living will always be prominent among them.

CHAPTER X

Own Homes for the Elderly

There is a myth of our time, widely current even among the reasonably well informed, according to which one of the side effects of the Welfare State has been to bundle into institutions old people who, previously, would have ended their lives, happy and well cared for, in the bosom of their devoted families. This regrettable change is due partly to the natural tendency of bureaucracy to herd individuals together and categorize them neatly, partly to the sudden atrophy of qualities like family affection and filial duty. Before any discussion of the services which the NOPWC, through its member bodies, is seeking to provide or to initiate for old people, it may be well to stress that the proportion of those aged sixty-five and over who are in residential homes or hospitals of any kind is less than 5 per cent. (These figures and those immediately following are given by Peter Townsend and Dorothy Wedderburn, *The Aged in the Welfare State*, 1965.) Of that 5 per cent, more than half are either bedfast or severely incapacitated. About one third of the total are unmarried. Just over one quarter of those who are married are childless and another two fifths have only one child. In all, 49 per cent of old people in institutions are childless, compared with 24 per cent of those living at home. So much for the myth. There is little doubt that, here and there, families are only too ready to unload their elderly relatives into 'free' homes or long-stay hospitals. There is none at all that, before such provision was available, there were many who kept their elderly relatives at home, with considerable hardship for both parties, either because of the scandal attached to having a parent in the workhouse (and the known bleakness of many workhouses) or to the inability to meet the maintenance charges which would have been asked from their families.

Overwhelmingly, then, it is towards old people living at home that, over the past twenty-five years, work for them has been directed. The achievement during that time has been admirably described by Mrs B. Shenfield, Visiting Lecturer in Sociology, Bedford College, when, addressing the NOPWC conference of 1960, which dealt with the care of the elderly, she imagined how one might explain it to an intelligent foreign visitor. 'We should say,' suggested Mrs Shenfield, 'that we aim to keep older people, whenever possible, living independently in their own homes, and that to make this possible we have provided, in addition to pension plans and free medical care, domiciliary services such as home nursing and home helps, meals on wheels, night attendance and laundry, shopping services and mobile libraries and a good deal of informal friendly visiting; while for the more mobile we provide clubs and day centres, workshops and holiday schemes, and, to keep as many old people as possible literally able to stand on their own feet we have subsidised chiropody treatment, both in people's own homes and in centres. We should tell our interested visitor that, in 1959, 22 per cent of local authority building was in the form of one-bedroom dwellings suitable for the small households of older people, and that when finally it becomes impossible for the elderly to maintain their own homes any longer, they can be cared for in small communal homes, with the minimum of rules and restrictions.'

It is a heartening picture, and accurate besides, as far as it goes. Mrs Shenfield went further. The provision of domiciliary services, whether by voluntary or statutory bodies, was, she said, very uneven throughout the country. Most areas had some services; few had all, and comprehensive care remained an unattained ideal in many areas. 'We know that old people are receiving a large share of the services of home nurses and home helps, but of all old people in England and Wales, about 4 per cent are receiving service from home helps. It sounds a tremendous achievement to organize the delivery to old people in their own homes of some one and a half million hot meals annually – and indeed it is a most praiseworthy effort – but it represents only the delivery of an average of two meals per week to about 20,300 people, a mere 0.3 per cent of the elderly. . . . There are two and a half as many cases being dealt with by home helps now as in 1948, but there are still difficulties in supplying the long-term needs of the elderly for domestic help; in this service, as in so many others, we are running to a standstill. Nowhere is this more clear than in the provision of residential care. . . . The numbers accommodated in local authority homes, or those provided by authorities through the agency of voluntary bodies, increased between 1948 and 1958 by 6·8 per cent. But the increase in the number of persons aged seventy-five and over in the same period was 27 per cent. . . . Even the present situation is maintained only by keeping nearly 34,000 beds, about half of those which local authorities have at their disposal, in large old institutions most of which everybody would like to see replaced.'

The intervening years have, of course, brought changes in the figures, but it would be idle to pretend that they have made any radical change in the overall picture. In its annual report for the year ended September 30, 1965, the National Corporation for the Care of Old People noted that there was still 'a large unmet need' for various types of housing for the aged and that the shortage of accommodation would increase in future years unless voluntary organizations could provide 'far more' dwellings than they were then providing. It was clear that local authorities alone were unlikely to be able to meet the whole need. Two years later, in its annual report for the year ended September 30, 1967, the National Corporation was suggesting that there had, for many years, been 'a gross under-estimate', if indeed any estimate at all had been made, of the total requirements in housing for old people. 'It can be shown,' says the report, 'that the proportion of new one-bedroom dwellings has been decreasing since 1963, though this does not necessarily imply that smaller numbers of dwellings are being built; indeed, in recent years, the total number of dwellings of this kind built annually has slowly increased, which is encouraging. But the waiting lists and, in some places, the attitude of the local authorities still suggest that the scale of need and the approach to the problem is not sufficiently well understood. . . . The Corporation would like to see a better understanding of old people by all, not just some, housing authorities. The old cannot be hustled; they do not always realize their rights. . . . The old sometimes see difficulty where, to a younger person, there is none. Housing for the old, as the Corporation said in its annual report last year, is a social service. There is more to be provided by the good authority than just dwellings.'

In 1967 also, in a report on private homes for old people, the National Corporation comments: 'It is generally agreed that there is an urgent need now for more places in homes for old people and that it shows little sign of decreasing in the immediate future, and many local authorities already have long waiting lists for admission to their homes.' Much the same might be said of the domiciliary services.

To make the point at the outset of the second part of this book, which will treat in rather more detail some of the different aspects of our provision for the elderly, is to be neither defeatist nor denigratory. Rather it is to show that nobody is less complacent than those most actively concerned in the work, but that, at the same time, they have cause to feel heartened as they glance back over twenty-five years. Occasionally, to 'look on this picture, and then on this' is a restoring exercise.

Housing is a case in point. The present 'unmet need' for various types of housing suitable for old people is, indeed, all too likely to continue if not to increase. It should be remembered, also, that large numbers of the relatively active elderly do not seek or need a flat or bungalow which is part of a group planned specifically as 'old people's housing', which may offer certain communal facilities and have a resident warden. They want convenient small dwellings, which, typically, particularly in towns, today means a one bed-roomed flat, and here they are in competition with young couples who are looking for just such accommodation to start their married lives. The public recognition that there is another group of old people who need housing specially adapted to their limitations or handicaps if they are to continue living in independence and some degree of comfort, is, relatively, a modern growth. Before World War II the only substantial provision for the housing of old people was made by the almshouse foundations, many of them venerable indeed, which offered accommodation for about 35,000. Since, in general, they were intended for the poor, aged or not – the fact that so often the two conditions went together is an eloquent comment on the position of the elderly in society – and for the most part had been built long before there was any idea of adapting houses to the needs of their occupants, many of them had break-neck stairs and fairly primitive plumbing. But the concept of independence within a group was a sound one, which persists in today's schemes, with which it was linked through the efforts of some of the nineteenth-century philanthropists to provide housing by voluntary enterprise.

Again, most of this was not intended particularly for the old. One of the earliest bodies in the field was the Labourers' Friend Society, whose 'model dwellings', besides benefiting their tenants, drew public attention to the scandalous character of much of the housing of the period and the general improvement in what today would be called social behaviour which could be effected by decent conditions. At the seventh national conference of the NOPWC, held in Bournemouth in 1954, Mr P. Leigh-Breese, Secretary, the Guinness Trust, recalled that the Labourers' Friend, re-named the Society for Improving the Conditions of the Labouring Classes, was still active. One of its earliest blocks was named Thanksgiving Buildings in gratitude for the deliverance from the cholera epidemic of 1849, which is a sharp reminder of the distance public health has travelled in less than 125 years. The latter half of the century saw the founding of several more housing trusts–the Peabody Donation Fund in 1882, the Guinness Trust in 1889, the Sutton Dwellings Trust in 1900, to be followed in 1906 by the Samuel Lewis Trust. By the mid-twentieth century, between them, they were providing accommodation for 70,000 people, with a proportion of the elderly among them. But the first effort intended solely for them was made in 1869 by a voluntary organization then known as Homes for Aged Poor (now the Harrison Homes), which opened 'flatlet houses' for them. Later other trusts, often intended for the benefit of former members of some particular trade or profession, set up groups of bungalows for old people.

In general, however, it was a wide-open field which the pioneers of voluntary housing associations entered between the two world wars. As in so many departments of social history, the record is one in which the efforts of individuals–often colourful ones–and the development of already established organizations reinforce each other.

The Church Army Housing Society was first registered as a Public Utility Society in 1924, so that it could help with the housing of the large and overcrowded family by building houses and flats for which low rents were charged. When the Second World War temporarily stopped new building the society began to buy up fairly large old houses and adapt them into bed-sitting rooms for the elderly. So began what was known as the Churchill Housing Scheme, which Miss D. E. Richardson, secretary of Church Army Housing Ltd described at the second national conference of the NOPWC in 1947. It enabled the tenants to preserve their independence against a background of security provided by a resident superintendent, or 'house mother' as she was then called, who was herself often a 'young elderly' retired nurse or Church Army Sister. One of the great strengths of the scheme was the attention paid to the kind of detail which was to become commonplace in housing for the elderly – handrails to baths, the placing of electric switches and so on – but which, at that time, could not be taken for granted. Costs would raise a bitter smile today. Miss Richardson told her audience that, recently, they had soared, 'one house had cost £2,200, with another £2,800 for adaptation'. Miss M. Merrylees, who became Secretary of the National Federation of Societies, had learned as a social worker of the acute need for suitable housing – indeed of housing of almost any kind – for old people, and, linking past with present, had found room for some of them in the very Thanksgiving Buildings in Grays Inn built after 1849. Mrs Margaret Neville Hill drew on two generations of experience of social work. Her mother was a Guardian in Cambridge, and, as a child, she saw something both of workhouse conditions and of the public attitude to those who might need to be lodged there. Thirty years later she herself became a Guardian, in a Middlesex borough, and, during her visiting, saw pensioners housed as cheaply as possible, in one basement or attic room, in the one case suffering from damp, in the other toiling up and down stairs with buckets of water. Rare indeed were the rooms which had running water on the same floor or any cooking arrangement other than an oil stove. With the help and encouragement of the Town Clerk, Mrs Hill, in 1933, decided to form a Public Utility Company for the conversion of houses into small suitable flats for old people and for some very poor families. The Borough Council agreed to lend 85 per cent of the cost of the reconditioned houses at a low rate of interest; the first committee had a rather 'do-it-yourself' flavour since it comprised a builder, an accountant, a lawyer and several social workers who were willing to do the rent collecting. Formalities in those days were at a minimum, which made for speed, and rents for rooms with water, sinks and small kitchenettes were around five shillings a week, including rates. From the first it was insisted that they should pay their way. So was born the Hornsey Housing Trust. Mrs Hill turned her attention to homes for old people, and notably to establishing the homes for the mentally frail old which bear her name.

Miss Olive Matthews began what was to be her life's work almost by chance, when, upon the death of her father, a Gloucestershire squire, she was faced with the task of providing a reasonable old age for servants who had worked on the estate for more than forty years. She campaigned persistently for better conditions for old people in institutions, insisting among other things, on their right to pocket money, and, as a shareholder in various companies, made a practice of attending their annual meetings in order to get up and ask the directors how they provided for their former employees. Her particular advocacy was for what was known as the 'Plus Granny' flat, that is an extra room, with connecting bathroom, added to an existing dwelling so that an elderly relative could be accommodated without too much strain on either side. Both Mrs Hill and Miss Matthews were members of the NOPWC and both, in their different ways, were examples of an essentially English breed of social reformers.

In the early nineteen thirties Miss Matthews was declaring that from 15 to 20 per cent of the flats on every housing estate should be deigned with the special needs of the old in mind and reserved for them alone. In fact, according to a statement by the Parliamentary Secretary to the Ministry of Health in 1938, only 1 per cent of the dwellings provided by local authorities since 1919 had been specifically deigned for old people who then made up 10 per cent of the population.

In 1947 the Seebohn Rowntree Committee, which studied the needs of the elderly, suggested a figure of 5 per cent. At present, when there remains a backlog of need to cut down, about 25 per cent of local authority building programmes is directed to the old. The need for specially designed houses for old people – as distinct from small houses – is, of course, withering comment on much of our standard design. Badly placed light switches and meters, casement windows that open outwards instead of inwards for easy cleaning, steep stairs with no hand-rail and high-sided baths with slippery bottoms are grossly inconvenient for tenants of any age, even if they are less likely to be lethal to those who remain active. Exposed water pipes are lunatic in a climate which brings several hard frosts each winter; the inadequacy of the heating system in many houses and blocks of flats had played its part in making Britain a nation of bronchitics long before medical research into hypothermia (deadly cold) in recent years had given wide publicity to the fact that low indoor temperatures were responsible for the deaths of many old people.

From earliest days, once the exigencies of wartime were over, housing was one of the chief concerns of the NOPWC. The first edition of *Old People's Welfare*, published in 1946, contained, besides plans of two suitable designs for housing for old people, notes on the desirable features of such accommodation and a declaration that housing for old people must form part of the housing schemes of every local authority. Under the existing legislation it was not compulsory for them to make this provision, and the NOPWC regretted that many of them had made none. A second edition of the booklet, published in the following year, quoted with approval the enterprise of Hornsey Borough Council, which was building thirty-four cottages of one room, including a large bed alcove with a window, kitchenette and bathroom. Two of the chosen tenants had lost their homes in the bombing. Of the rest, six were leaving six-roomed houses, eleven, five-roomed houses, another eleven four-roomed houses and four three-roomed houses. It was a striking example of how much could be done to house families if the elderly were given an alternative to houses which were too big for their needs and capacities. In that same year, 1946, the first national conference of the NOPWC heard from an architect speaker, Mr Edward Arnstrong, of housing provision for the old in Scandinavia, where the concept of housing in flats or grouped bungalows where there was some discreet supervision, with support when needed, also, possibly, the opportunity of taking main meals in a common dining-room, was well established. It throws an incidental light on the progress which twenty years has seen at least in publicly expressed attitudes towards the old.

One delegate asked whether there were any facilities for dealing with 'cantankerous old people'. Mr Moss, who was presiding at the session, replied that when he had visited Sweden, he had been told that 'any difficult cases are threatened with being sent to an institution in Stockholm if they become unmanageable'.

At this time the emphasis was necessarily on conversion rather than on new building, and the pattern of the Churchill Housing Scheme was adopted by a number of organizations, among them the Women's Voluntary Service. So far as can be discovered, the first local authority to provide housing for the elderly in the form of a group of purpose-built bungalows with a resident warden, was Sturminster Newton, in Dorset. Such an initiative in a predominantly agricultural county is an incidental reminder that the housing needs of the elderly in the country, though they are necessarily on a smaller scale than in the towns, may be even more acute, both because the standard of their existing housing may be primitive and because they are often too far off the beaten track to profit from aids like Home Helps and Meals on Wheels. Dorset made the discovery, later to be confirmed time and again, that old people properly housed and within reach of friendly help were for the most part able to continue in their own homes until the end of their lives. This is the type of provision on which voluntary bodies, other than the established philanthropic and charitable Housing Trusts, are increasingly concentrating.

There are many variations on the formula, more or less provision for communal services and communal living, bungalows, purpose-built flats or converted houses. Whichever is chosen or dictated by the particular circumstances, each tenant is able to communicate direct with the warden's dwelling, usually by means of a push bell, though recently there has been some exploration of the possibilities of an inter-com system. There is general agreement, in principle at least, that such accommodation for old people should form a small unit within a normal section of the population, rather than that large numbers of the elderly should be herded in what can become a compound for the over-sixties, and that they should be centrally placed, rather than on the outskirts of a town, far from pub and church and cinema, Post Office and chemist and bus stop. It is recognized, too, that the personality of the warden, more than any other single factor, affects the happiness of the tenants. A warden, as the NOPWC has taken pains to make clear, is neither a janitor, nor a nanny, nor a home help. Her job – or theirs, for there are some husband-and-wife posts – is to provide background security.

Increasingly, voluntary bodies are forming themselves into Housing Associations, which enables them to meet rather specialized needs in a way which is hardly possible for a housing authority. Housing Associations are recognized as charitable organizations and qualify for an exchequer subsidy, which normally makes a difference of something less than 10s a week in the rent which they charge. They must obtain their finance – other than any which may be provided by public benevolence – through the local authorities concerned. The latter vary in their response; there has in the past been some evidence that there are authorities which seemed unaware of their powers in this direction, and so caused delay in the procedure. But though it is entirely possible that the system of financing could be improved it is, at present, the best one we have got for the purpose, and the NOPWC, directly and indirectly, has done a great deal to stimulate the setting up of housing associations.

Housing Societies, which are not charitable organizations, though they must be non profit-making, do not qualify for the Exchequer subsidy, and obtain their finance from the Government sponsored Housing Corporation. Some have been formed to cater for those of the elderly who can afford to pay modest economic rents but who, otherwise, would have no hope of finding pleasant quarters within their means. There is room for more of this kind of provision. There is room, indeed, and there will be in any foreseeable future, for more of every possible kind of provision if the ideal of old people's being able to live comfortably in their own homes is to be a reality. It is more often than not overlooked that, for between 90,000 and 100,000 people over sixty-five, 'their own home' means a hotel, a boarding house, a hostel or a common lodging house (Townsend and Wedderburn: *The Aged in the Welfare State*). Besides the many who live with their children or other relatives, there are a small number who have been found substitute families by means of the boarding out schemes run by some voluntary organizations.

On this, it is interesting to note that it was being mentioned as long ago as 1949. At the National Conference of the NOPWC in the autumn of that year Mr G. E. (later Sir George) Haynes, presiding at an open forum, suggested that more people should be encouraged to board the elderly. A speaker from Ipswich said that the local OPWC had many applications for lodgings and thought that local committees could set up registers of suitable accommodation. He added that it was essential that they should be visited and supervised and that one of the chief difficulties in the idea was what would happen if the old people became ill.

Four or five years later two Councils of Social Service in the West Country, Exeter and Plymouth, were finding out what did happen. The first scheme started almost fortuitously when the Exeter council received the offer of a home for an old person at a time when they were concerned about an elderly man due to be discharged from hospital who had nowhere suitable to go. Even in face of what seemed a happy solution the council was careful to arrange a meeting between hostess and prospective guest before taking up the offer. The old man stayed in his new home until his death two years later. Plymouth, having received many applications from old people looking for accommodation, placed an advertisement in a local paper and got twenty-one replies. This was in 1954, which seems to make these two towns the pioneers of boarding out schemes, though Hampshire County Council, whose revised scheme, employing a geriatric social worker, dates from 1963, had begun to explore the possibilities of boarding out in 1952.

In their early stages both the Exeter and the Plymouth schemes were supported by a grant from the National Corporation for the Care of Old People, which made possible the appointment of a full-time organizer. The vital lesson demonstrated was that careful placement was essential to success and that it was a time-consuming job. Three weeks is the minimum time which, it is estimated, is needed to 'match' hostess and boarder and make the necessary arrangements, and two or three cases is as many as most boarding out officers can manage at one time. So the need for adequate funds to pay a worker, besides providing for clerical help and other expenses is paramount. Given the necessary resources, human and financial, the results achieved can be impressive, as is shown by the development of the idea. By 1964 the NOPWC had twenty-nine boarding out schemes recorded, some of which were organized by Old People's Welfare Committees, others by local authorities. One of the largest was that administered by the Old People's Welfare Committee in North-West Kent, which employed seven part-time officers and received grants from the county council and from five of the eight local councils concerned. During the year it had made ninety-four new placings, besides arranging some short-stay and holiday accommodation. Lewisham started a scheme at the end of 1961, the annual cost of about £400 being included in the Borough Council's general grant to the OPW Association. By the end of 1965 it had made fifty-five permanent placings. Flintshire County Council started a scheme in 1956, and, by 1965, had found permanent homes for 318 people and arranged short stay care for another seventy.

At Colchester, Essex, the psycho-geriatric unit of Severalls Hospital began successfully to board out patients who were homeless and without interested relatives but who did not need hospital treatment. It was planned to extend the scheme to old people who had not entered hospital, or who were attending as day patients.

Boarding out is not a method which can ever be expected to solve the problems of large numbers, but for the very reason that it is essentially a personal service, it can make an enormous contribution to human happiness. One of the most rewarding experiences for organizers has been to see elderly boarders settle into homes where they remain until their deaths. It is often a preferred alternative for those of the elderly who, perhaps because they have had jobs which did not allow them to set up a home of their own, have no taste for housekeeping and no wish to live in even the most comfortable bungalow or flatlet on their own.

Such is the variety of the living arrangements of the 95 per cent of our old people who are living within the community, some of whom are enabled to remain within it by the complex of services provided by statutory and voluntary bodies which will be looked at more closely in the next chapter.

CHAPTER XI

Services for Care at Home

The National Corporation for the Care of Old People, already mentioned more than once, came into being in 1947 as the creation of the Nuffield Foundation. At that time it was financed partly by the Foundation, partly by grants from the Lord Mayor of London's National Air Raid Distress Fund. The latter, of course, continued for only a few years. Its objects, 'to promote the welfare of the aged in such ways as might seem desirable to the Governors to meet current needs' are, at first sight, so similar to those of the National Old People's Welfare Council, whose terms of reference are 'To study the needs of old people and to encourage and promote measures for their well being' that members of the public are often pardonably confused about their respective functions. In fact the distinctions are clear and go beyond the fact that the National Corporation is a grant-providing organization, while the NOPWC has no funds of any consequence to dispose of. Before all else the NOPWC is a co-ordinating body, and a national centre for information and advice on all aspects of the care of the elderly. Fifty or so national voluntary organizations, half a dozen Government departments and Old People's Welfare Committees in all parts of the country are represented on it. Its influence in helping to create an informed public opinion and its action in prodding Government Departments as necessary have been already described.

The National Corporation, in the first twenty years of its existence, has made available in the service of old age more than £2½ million, and continues to make grants, mostly in relatively small sums to voluntary organizations throughout the country. Its policy, however, has developed very considerably since the early years when it was chiefly concerned in making grants to organizations who were trying to meet the acute need for accommodation for old people. When the first rush of applications slowed down it was able to devote more time to collecting information at first hand about work for old people in various parts of the country, which, in its turn, had an influence upon its own policy. Today it is concerned above all to support new ideas which local bodies have evolved in the light of their own experience of needs, particularly when they promise to be generally applicable and to fill a gap in the statutory services. In practice this means that it makes its own judgment about current priorities in deciding which of a number of applications for grant aid it shall meet.

It may be assumed that, had the National Corporation been founded before August, 1947, it and not the Nuffield Foundation would have published a book which has done more than any other single work to focus public attention on, indeed, at that time, to create public awareness of, the circumstances, the character, the needs of old people living at home, whether alone or with relatives. Dr J. H. Sheldon's *The Social Medicine of Old Age*, a survey of 583 men and women of pensionable age living in Wolverhampton was, at the time, a revelation of what could be done for the well-being of those who were putting up, for the most part cheerfully, with disabilities which, in another sphere of life, would have been quickly remedied. That it should have disclosed a large number of medical conditions requiring, but not receiving treatment, was to be expected. This was before the establishment of the National Health Service, and, as later research has shown, even when medical care is freely available, it cannot always be assumed that the elderly will take their complaints to the doctor. What was equally striking was the need for teeth and spectacles and hearing aids, for chiropody and various forms of physiotherapy and help with the house-work and the washing. Sixteen years later, in 1963, the National Corporation was to publish a book, *The Ageing Countryman*, by Dr H. C. Miller, which did for the elderly people of a Welsh border area what Dr Sheldon's had done for townspeople, and, in doing so, effectively shattered any remaining illusions about there being no need for public schemes of care in the country because neighbourly help could be counted on. Even if it could, there would remain those whose homes are so isolated that, effectively, they have no neighbours.

During the twenty years which have passed since the publica-

tion of *The Social Medicine of Old Age*, statutory and voluntary organizations between them, if they have not succeeded in
filling the gaps, have at least shown how, given the staff and
the money, it would be possible to fill them. Today the old, like
the rest of the population, can obtain hearing aids and properly
prescribed spectacles and, if they are sufficiently enterprising,
false teeth which fit at least approximately. When they are ill
they can be cared for at home by doctor and district nurse –
though both general practitioners and district nurses are over-
burdened.

In theory at least they can count on having small adaptations
like handrails, or a ramp over an awkward step, made in their
houses; they will be taken to and from hospital for physiotherapy; a chiropodist will attend to their painful feet; holidays
may be arranged for them; if they suffer from failing sight the
local library will supply large-print books, and, in any case,
will bring a library van to their door; if they find it difficult to
get in and out of the bath unaided an attendant will come round
to help; if they can no longer get to church visitors may bring
a tape-recording of a service and play it to them; if they can no
longer look after the garden a squad of schoolboys will take it
over and if cooking is too much for them a hot meal will appear
on their table at least five days a week. In practice, of course,
their chances of benefiting from these possibilities depend upon
where they live, since the means, as well as the energy and the
initiative of both local authorities and voluntary societies vary
greatly. Even in a district – if any exists – where there is no lack
of either money or workers, professional or voluntary, there
remains the problem of finding those who are in most urgent
need of the services offered. The arguments for and against
maintaining a register of all elderly people are still being
debated. While nothing of the kind exists the agencies through
which old people suffering various hardships and disabilities are
brought to the notice of those who can offer them help will
continue to range from the doctor to the milkman.

Among the whole complex of services – and excluding for the
moment that provided by general practitioner and district nurse
– there are four which are of cardinal importance in the lives
of old people, particularly those who live alone. Two are concerned with material, two with psychological well-being. They

are the Home Help Service, Meals on Wheels, voluntary visitors who bring something of the outside world into the restricted lives of many of the old and clubs of different kinds which take them into the outside world. Three of these are voluntary services and two should remain so. The fourth, the Home Help scheme, though it was from the first a statutory provision, can be augmented by volunteers.

Home Helps were originally recruited to take over the housework in confinement cases, and, strictly, mothers have first call on them. Nevertheless, today, more than four-fifths of the total number of people receiving their services in London are the aged and infirm and the chronic sick. The only serious complaint ever heard about the service is that it should be doubled certainly, and possibly trebled, and that it is ridiculous that a form of help which is a very lifeline for many old people should not operate on Sundays. A good Home Help – and very many, judged by standards other than those of mere domestic economy, are really admirable – does far more than maintain reasonable cleanliness and order in the sometimes unpromising quarters of those she cares for. She does a little shopping on the way in, puts the lunch on before she leaves, brings the local gossip, sometimes parks her youngest in his pushchair in the passage to the possibly rather fearful interest of the elderly householder and has been known to send her husband round to chop some wood or fix a dripping tap. It is the essentially human and homely character of this service which makes it so valuable. At its best it would be more accurate to describe it as a social service with an element of domestic cleaning than as rather haphazard charring, and it is possible that a recruiting campaign that stressed this aspect of service might have unexpected success. It is equally possible that if local authorities paid rates which were competitive with those current for private domestic work, which is often less taxing, they might find more takers. Some of them do offer extra inducements. The now extinct Middlesex County Council payed its Home Helps' travelling expenses and counted travelling time as working time; Surrey County Council allows an extra 10s for the first cleaning of a particularly neglected home, and has a special allowance of an extra fourpence per hour for the care of premises in unusually bad condition. Certain places, of course, have particularly difficult problems, either because they have a high proportion of old people, often living alone, as may happen in a central city area, from which most of the younger families have moved out to housing estates, or because there is a local tradition of work for women in factory or mill, with plenty of jobs available. Admitting all that, it is still unsatisfactory to see neighbouring local authorities in very similar areas planning for widely different numbers of Home Helps in proportion to their elderly population. It is particularly so when nothing leads one to suppose that authorities whose planned provision of Home Helps is only one-third of their neighbours' have thought the problem through to the extent of planning for an increased number of places in local authority homes to accommodate the old people who lack the help which would have allowed them to remain in their own homes. All the evidence points to the fact that many of the old who now receive the services of a Home Help need more frequent visits if their homes are to be kept comfortable, that for the number now served by local authority Home Helps there are as many again who would like to be (many of whom would certainly qualify to receive such help) and that investigation should reveal others who, though they might not ask for help, would certainly benefit from it. It is possible, too, that there are old people who will not admit to needing a Home Help because they do not realize that they will not be required to pay for the service if it is beyond their means.

Even at its best, the regular Home Help Service cannot meet all the needs of a frail elderly person, which are far more varied and irregular than that of having the house cleaned and scrubbed once weekly. They want what might familiarly be called a 'popping-in service', and popping-in, at regular intervals during the day, is what is provided for by the paid Good Neighbour scheme.

This was first tried in St Pancras, from September 1961 to March, 1963, with the support and co-operation of the Borough Council, the St Pancras Association for the Care of the Aged and other local bodies. A generous grant from the City Parochial Foundation made the experiment possible. It was based on the belief that many old people were not fit to be left alone for long at a time, and needed more care than could be provided by the existing District Nursing and Home Help services, but were not likely to be improved by hospital treatment, even if they wished to enter hospital and a bed could be found, and were not necessarily candidates for a residential home. The Oxford City Old People's Welfare Committee, helped by an anonymous donation, also ran a pilot scheme. Good Neighbours are now firmly established, the schemes being run sometimes by local authorities, sometimes by OPW committees. They offer an opportunity for the two to work together profitably.

Unlike a Home Help a Good Neighbour does not undertake household cleaning, though she (or, indeed, he, for this is a service which might well attract newly retired men) may undertake bed-making and a little cooking of the simpler sort. Its essence is several calls during the day – perhaps to get a morning cup of tea and start the fire, to do some shopping, to screw in securely the stopper of a hot water bottle which arthritic fingers cannot manage and to see that lights are out and doors locked at night. For this, obviously, the Good Neighbour must live close at hand. The small payment is a recognition that the helper has accepted responsibility for carrying out these tasks regularly and, incidentally, prevents a feeling of being 'put-upon' which can sometimes be experienced by the most good-hearted of neighbours when they find themselves responsible for more and more of an old friend's household jobs.

In some places, again by either local authority or voluntary committee, there has been provided a rather similar service of 'night sitting-in'. It is important not to confuse this with night nursing. Some who volunteer for it may be retired nurses in fact, but no nursing is involved. The job is one for a sensible woman, preferably with some experience of old people, who, by taking over the night watch can either ensure that an exhausted family have a regular break in their task of caring for a chronic invalid, or enable an old person who is living alone to be nursed at home when temporarily ill instead of having to go into hospital. Day sitters-in are an obvious development of this: one free day a week may be enough to stave off breakdown in a woman who is combining the duties of mother of a family and daughter of a parent who cannot be left alone for an hour.

While, in the majority of places, the regular Home Help service does not operate on Sundays, and usually only in reduced fashion on Saturday, this, too, is a gap which volunteers might

118

fill. The usual official alibi for this week-end shut-down of both
Home Help and meals services is that 'friends and relatives can
cope then'.

This is to show an almost wilful unawareness of the fact that
the most needy of the old have few friends and no relatives and
that, in an increasingly mobile age, some central areas can be
virtual deserts of loneliness on Sundays.

Meals on wheels, increasingly, are being provided by local
authorities, often with voluntary help in their delivery, instead
of by voluntary agencies assisted by local authorities. It is one
more example – chiropody services are another – of voluntary
bodies tracing a path which will later be converted into a broad
highway by statutory bodies, and, in this instance, it should
be particularly welcomed. One of the most striking facts disclosed in a report of an inquiry into meals on wheels for old
people conducted by the Government Social Survey and published in 1960 by the National Corporation for the Care of Old
People was that the number of meals needed was at least four
times as many as the number at that time being served. The
years between have brought an increase. Between 1965 and
1966, for instance, the wvs, the largest voluntary provider of
meals, raised its provision of meals from seven million to eight
million. But they have also brought an increase in the number
of old people, setting aside the fact that there is no reliable
source of information on how many old people actually need
meals delivered to their homes. Those who do need them,
because they are too frail, or possibly simply too discouraged
and lethargic to cook for themselves, often with inadequate
equipment, must certainly need them on more than the one
day a week, which is as often as some areas are able to provide
them. How do they manage when, as may happen, the service
shuts down for a few weeks in summer, because most of the
voluntary helpers are on holiday? What do they eat instead?
The survey found that, on days when meals were not delivered,
(excluding Sundays), the meals of only 23 per cent of older
people reached the recommended standard. Nearly one-quarter
of the total sample did not have any potatoes and more than
one-third did not have green vegetables, from which the report
assumed that many older people did not have at least one cooked
meal every day.

Another discovery was that the supply of meals was not necessarily related to the local demand. Often voluntary helpers were easier to recruit in fairly prosperous districts, whereas those where was to be found the highest concentration of the needy old had correspondingly fewer of the leisured who could help with the service. All these things point to the need for this service to be a statutory one. Voluntary help would continue to be welcomed, and voluntary helpers could take the opportunity of locating lonely old people who might benefit from other services which their different organizations could provide. Even in the brief contacts which they now make in serving meals, they win themselves an important place in the lives of their elderly customers, and there is no doubt of the personal quality of the relationship they establish. On this, the Survey's report records an occasion when Lady Reading, Chairman of the WRVS, who was acting as a server in place of an absent member, was greeted gruffly by an elderly man with: 'You're five minutes late – and not the right one!'

There remains in question the quality of the meals supplied. In fairness, the survey found that the overwhelming majority of the customers were satisfied with the content, the quantity and the cooking of the meals they got, also, on paper, a main course of meat or fish, with potatoes and another vegetable, with either soup before or a pudding afterwards, very occasionally, both, is dietetically adequate. Admittedly, too, the character of the meals and the standard of cooking vary from place to place. The fact remains that there are meals services where a check of the meals on the plate rather than on paper would show an overplus of stodge, a slender allowance of meat, and that often in some kind of made-up dish, a preponderance of dried peas and beans and a scanty allowance of the kind of 'afters' based on fresh fruit, or eggs or milk which are normally recommended for the elderly in more fortunate circumstances. While there are certain London boroughs with an Invalid Meals Service which can provide suitable dishes for those who have to follow a restricted diet, there are others where it is impossible to obtain a variant on the standard menu, which may have been based on the needs of a school kitchen or a works canteen, both common sources of supply for mobile meals. Usually things are better when the meals come from an Old People's Home in the neighbourhood: they should be better when they come from a hospital kitchen. For the future, perhaps the best prospect for appetizing meals, which would involve the disappearance of so-called 'green vegetables' which, too often, boil down to a wodge of cabbage which has been humped around town for an hour and a half before delivery and may be reheated before consumption, is the frozen meals which have already been tried in some districts.

The whole question of the nutrition of the elderly is at last getting the attention it deserves. The NOPWC has long been concerned about it and took every opportunity, direct and indirect, of urging upon the Ministry of Health the importance of establishing the basic dietary requirements for an older person. Its persistence has been rewarded by the setting up by the Ministry of Health Committee of the Panel on Nutrition of the Elderly, one of whose aims is to discover these dietary needs. A number of independent research projects have suggested that at present there are deficiencies in the diets of many of the old, including those in hospital. The cause is not always absolute poverty, though this comes high on the list. The old, and particularly old men, often have very little idea of what makes up a properly balanced diet and, sometimes, may cling to eating habits established earlier in life which were never good and become increasingly unsuitable as they age. Some have little cooking skill and many, particularly the solitary, lose the will to buy and cook food. The price of fresh fruit often limits its use; such factors as arthritic hands which may make it impossible for an old person to peel an orange can play their part in a deficiency of Vitamin C which can produce the signs of scurvy. At the 1966 National Conference of the NOPWC Dr A. N. Exton-Smith, Secretary of the British Geriatrics Society and Consultant Physician in the Geriatric Department of University College Hospital, London, referred to a survey instituted by the King Edward's Hospital Fund which had examined the diet of sixty elderly women living alone. It showed among other things that the intake of protein dropped sharply for the 'older old', particularly for the group over seventy-eight years old. One consequence of this was that, if they became bedridden, they were more liable to develop bed-sores.

Assuming that mobile meals are increasingly taken over by

local authorities, there will remain ample scope for voluntary bodies to find other ways of providing meals for those who are not necessarily either infirm or housebound, but who, left to themselves, would not have the minimum of one good meal a day, or who, perhaps, can manage their cooking on most days but would benefit greatly from the stimulus of something different occasionally. Luncheon clubs are one obvious solution, providing as they do an incentive to go out and the chance of making new acquaintances, with, for those who provide them, the chance of serving a better meal because, generally speaking, they are catering for smaller numbers than the mobile service and can serve them hot on the spot. Another might be to encourage neighbours to pool their resources, each cooking on alternate days for two, instead of for herself alone. For the more frail there might be an adaptation of the Good Neighbour scheme which involved an invitation to lunch on three or four days a week. In scattered rural areas it might be easier to enrol a few volunteer cooks who would visit old people in their homes to produce a meal for two or three than to transport all the old people to some distant central point. It is an area in which there is almost unlimited room for experiment and variety and where the opportunity of choice for the elderly customers is particularly important.

CHAPTER XII

Visiting and Clubs

A London District Nurse paid daily visits over a long period to an old lady living alone who had a badly ulcerated leg. At last her care and skill were rewarded – the ulcer healed. The nurse went off on holiday, allowing herself to indulge in a little justifiable professional pride.

When, three weeks later, she returned to duty, the old lady's name was first on her list of calls for the day. The ulcer had broken down again and they were back in square one, with daily calls and dressings. It was a week before the nurse found out the cause. The old lady had deliberately scratched the newly-healed ulcer because, now that there was no need for the daily visit of a district nurse, nobody came to see her at all.

At its worst, that is the kind of reality behind the finding of a recent Mass Observation survey that loneliness, along with lack of money, was the biggest problem which old people had to face. Not only is it in itself a problem, it is at least a contributory cause of many other problems, among them suspicion, apathy towards such services as may be available, and the kind of inertia which leads to self-neglect. When it does not seem worth while to get proper meals for yourself, or to change in the afternoon because nobody is likely to call, it is relatively a short step to malnutrition and a state when, from ceasing to clean your room or flat very much, you cease to wash yourself very much, if at all.

Organized visiting schemes for the elderly and clubs for the elderly are two ways of combating loneliness, which should not necessarily be equated with solitude. There are many solitaries who are not lonely and, possibly, even more of the elderly who are desperately lonely even when living with relatives. Both are eminently suitable activities to be organized by voluntary bodies and carried out by voluntary workers. In some ways, indeed, they are better done by voluntary workers than by professionals, though not, one need hardly say, because of any lack of human qualities in the latter. Visiting schemes need no large capital outlay. Yet visiting has been described as 'the Cinderella of the old people's welfare services', often languishing in areas where clubs of various kinds are thriving. The two should complement each other. There are some club members who would, or do benefit also from a friendly visitor. There are some lifelong unclubables whose only hope of being kept in touch with the world is by way of somebody who will come and seek them out at home since they are by nature non-joiners.

It is possible that two factors may be largely responsible for the deficiencies of visiting schemes. The first is that a number of people are unable to decide precisely what a visiting scheme should try to do. Is it a means of providing opportunities for a more or less regular friendly chat to an elderly person who, in the normal way, gets little company and is, if not housebound, at least limited in the extent to which she can get about? Or is it a system of keeping a regular watch on those of the elderly who, because of great frailty, or unsuitable housing, or difficulties of temperament of one sort or another, seem likely to become social casualties, in which case it demands of the visitor not only a fair amount of skill but the ability and willingness to write regular reports? The other is the idea that, since paying a spontaneous friendly visit on another person is a normal human activity, there is no need to go to any great trouble about organizing it. The combined results are that some schemes may fall between two stools, that some potentially most valuable visitors may be deterred because the whole thing sounds too professional and difficult for them, and that, with no possible doubt, there exist visiting services whose administration is chaotic and which keep on their roll both visitors and old persons who exist on paper only.

The answer to the first problem is that a visiting scheme is or should be, both a source of friendship and company and a means of ensuring that solitary old people do not fall through the network of the social services, either because they are not known to the services or because they do not know of the existence of the services. On the one level visiting is an operation of replacement which seeks to ascertain the practical and material needs of old people and provide what is lacking, or see that it is provided. On another, equally vital, it tries to meet the emotional needs which spring from deprivation, insecurity and loneliness on a personal level.

The most convincing contradiction to the second idea is the evidence that the most successful visiting schemes are those which have an organizer rather than being run as one of the several activities of a local Old People's Welfare Committee. There has been a recent striking example at Wolverhampton, where, for many years, the Old People's Welfare Council has run a small visiting scheme. A grant from the National Corporation for the Care of Old People made it possible to appoint an organizer. The result was that, in 1967, Wolverhampton had a comprehensive service under which some 500 old people were visited regularly, either weekly or fortnightly, while others were looked up as a safeguard at longer intervals. There were 300 volunteers to do the visiting. It was a grant from the National Corporation also which led to the development of the most effective visiting scheme in the rural area of Louth, Lincolnshire, which illustrates the value of such a service in country districts where isolation for the old is often geographical, not merely social. Leeds, in 1966, obtained grants from the Sembal and Stembridge Trusts, which made possible a similar appointment. Elsewhere, local authorities have included in their administrative grant the salary of a full-time or part-time organizer. The first in the field here is believed to have been Hull City Welfare Services Committee, which appointed a full-time visiting organizer who was seconded to duties with the Hull Council for Old People's Welfare.

There are excellent arguments in favour of an organizer's being responsible to a voluntary body. Friendly visiting is not a statutory service, it is a community responsibility. But there are equally excellent reasons why she should work in close and amicable co-operation with the officers of the local authority. Each has something to give and something to learn from the other and, at different times, an old person is likely to need the help of both. Indeed the training of both should have the same fundamental content, though obviously at different levels. That voluntary visitors need training is now generally recognized. They must know what services are available locally and make sure that those whom they visit know of them too; even today there are many of the elderly who have not heard of the existence of amenities like Meals on Wheels or luncheon clubs. Visitors must learn also to be aware of details like an unguarded fire, an awkward stair with no handrail, or simple needs like somebody to collect a pension on wet days. They need some information about old age, its limitations, its occasional eccentricities and the changes it can bring in character, as well as physical attributes. Many wish they were told a little more about the onset of senile dementia, not only of the danger signals but of what they should in fact do or say when an old friend tells them seriously that somebody has stolen four pairs of merino blankets from the chest on the landing, or something equally startling and improbable. It might be argued that acceptable attitudes cannot be taught, but that is perhaps a little unfair. Some thought in matching visitor to visited helps here. It is not kind to either side to send a visitor whose life has been sheltered and whose social experience correspondingly limited to an old person whose home is neglected to the point of being upsetting to the fastidious. Training courses all stress the point that a Lady Bountiful attitude is a capital mistake, but perhaps they might carry it even further. There can be few less engaging ways of approaching an isolated elderly person than by saying in effect: 'I know you are lonely so I thought you would like me to come to see you.' Few people are ready to admit to being lonely, which they see, however obscurely, as a social or personal failure.

A first visit, if at all possible, should have a tangible objective, whether it is delivering a copy of the parish magazine or bringing news of the opening of a luncheon club in the neighbourhood. Beyond that the visitor who conveys the idea that he or she is new in the district and would be glad to find a welcoming friend, or is overworked and harassed and longing for an occasional half-hour of peace, or has recently lost a parent, or is separated from family by distance, and so glad of the company of an older person, has got off on the right foot. If all voluntary visitors have written on their hearts a reminder that they are self-invited guests in somebody else's house, if they have the normal degree of human warmth and if they bear in mind that good manners will ease many situations they should have no grave difficulties. The late Dorothy Keeling was fond of contrasting two old people's visitors whom she knew in her youth. The one was a social worker who, when visiting The Poor, always carried with her a sheet of brown paper which she used to spread on a chair before sitting on it. The other was the local mayoress, a woman of breeding as well as intelligence, who, when she called on an old person, left a card as she would have done on her other friends (this was before two world wars). She, clearly, needed no teaching on the essentials.

Apart from the differences between individual visitors, which will be as great as those of the old people whom they visit, there are different kinds of visits, or visits for different purposes. At the 1966 national conference of the NOPWC a doctor who was organizing a visiting service for his county suggested that a comprehensive service should have four kind of visitors, 'odd-jobbers', who might be school-children, who could paint a room, or do shopping, or chop firewood; 'friendliness and companionship' visitors, mainly retired people, case workers who would be probably local authority, who solved problems and tried to give material help, and, finally, 'diagnostic visitors'. These last should be special workers attached to a general practitioner who could diagnose the social, medical and welfare condition of an old person and pay regular visits to everybody over sixty-five in the area.

The last is much the kind of work already done by the Health Visitors to old people who exist in some areas, also by the social workers who are attached to general practitioners. The first are still relatively few, the second rare indeed. In present circumstances most voluntary visiting schemes will have to lean heavily on the more skilled of its own helpers, who may have had experience of old people and who will receive a more strenuous training. Matching visitor to old person and skill to need is one of the paramount tasks of the visiting organizer, but first comes the basic one of recruiting. The striking increase in numbers which usually follows the appointment of an organizer whose sole responsibility is the visiting scheme shows how much can be done here. Successful organizers usually find that a variety of methods can be used – advertising in local papers, putting notices in shop windows, giving talks to church or club groups. The last has the advantage of enabling obviously unsuitable aspirants to be tactfully diverted into other channels.

Finding the old people who need to be visited is the other side of the picture. The survey into visiting schemes which Miss W. M. Bayes (now Mrs Copeman) carried out for the NOPWC in 1964 suggested that the normal proportion of old people needing visiting normally ranges from one in fifteen to one in twenty, which, in a good-sized city, represents a very considerable number. Finding them is seldom difficult once a visiting service is well publicized. Some 'refer' themselves to it, other referrals may come from anyone from a statutory officer to the milkman. It is the organizer who must assess need, find the most suitable visitor for a given old person, and, perhaps most important, see that 'dear old ladies' do not get a plethora of visits while the withdrawn, outwardly unwelcoming and most needy may be neglected. This is where record-keeping is vital. The 1964 survey showed that there was no one type of organization which was 'best' for every visiting scheme. Miss Bayes, who obtained details from twenty-four reorganizations and studied ten of them in detail, found that some were centrally organized, others worked through groups attached to churches or voluntary organizations, others were organized on a ward basis. The essential is that records should be kept and that the co-operation between all concerned should be a reality.

One heartening fact is that the range of 'suitable' visitors is wide indeed. Nowadays the middle-aged, middle-class woman with a social conscience and a good deal of leisure, valuable as she is, makes up only a small part of the spectrum. At one end of the scale the 'young elderly', in particular the newly retired, men as well as women, can often give much to the old. Some firms, among them Esso and Unilever, have organized schemes by which they visit older retired employees. At the other end, increasingly, young people are interesting themselves in helping the elderly, sometimes as members of voluntary societies, sometimes as a school activity. Very occasionally, in some of the last-named schemes, one catches a hint of something that is at least as undesirable as Lady Bountiful patronage – a regarding of service to the elderly as part of the syllabus for 'civics', with the corollary that the chief function of the elderly is to provide an opportunity for the young to cultivate social virtues. Fortunately the boys and girls themselves can almost always be relied upon to rise above this. Too much should not be asked of them, but the practical jobs which are obviously suitable for them to do in groups are not all they have to offer. Many old people take pleasure in the stimulus, the change, the sheer fun which the company of young people, in duly measured doses, can provide, and it may come from unexpected quarters. To meet, coming down the stairs leading to an old friend's flat, a pair of adolescents wearing the utmost that Carnaby Street can do, and to be told a moment later that 'you must have just met my boys. They come quite often to take me for a walk in the park and I always feel so safe with them because they know I'm tottery so they hold on tight' is to receive a salutary jolt to preconceived ideas. If the ideas happen to include any about the narrowness of the elderly they too will be shattered when the old lady goes on to say that she is so interested in the clothes her escorts wear. This week they both had their floral shirts. Last week one had 'a most beautiful red silk tunic like an Indian one, and white trousers with it'.

A good visiting service is one which, making the most of this variety, builds up around a core of the specially skilled and experienced who take on the difficult cases a much larger number of recruits each of whom has been helped to realize that, whatever practical help they may give to the elderly, there are two intangibles which are even more valuable. The first is, not simply the provision of incident in an otherwise monotonous life, but the provision of additional mental furniture. A simple measure of well-being is whether or not one has something nice to think about in the ten minutes before dropping off to sleep. When the day has offered only solitude between four walls, and tomorrow promises to be like yesterday, there is little alternative to taking refuge in a progressively distant past. When a visitor has come, there is not only the occasion itself to be gone over in detail, there are matters arising. What name will the visitor's brother and sister-in-law finally choose for the new baby? What colour hat will she decide to wear for the christening? Will she take the old person's advice that rose pink becomes her? Of such trivia is daily life made up. Lacking them it may wither.

The second and more important of the intangibles is the gift of personal concern which only the voluntary helper can give. If they are to survive, professionals, who, in this context, include doctors and clergy as well as social workers, must avoid involvement with individuals; they can continue to supply the needs of large numbers only by practising a detached kindness. The volunteer is there to be involved; the one or two old people whom she visits are personal friends on whom she is free to bestow personal affection. The amount of it that is awakened in return is often humbling.

Personal concern is the justification for one section of visiting which is often overlooked, that of some of the old who live with relatives and of many who live in homes or in the geriatric wards of hospitals. Obviously, in the two latter instances at least, there is no question of keeping an eye on their physical well-being, which is being taken care of professionally. But it may very well be that a visitor offers their one chance of holding on to their individuality. He or she may be their single contact with the world outside, their one source of a birthday card to be displayed on their locker, or a postcard from Morecambe or Positano, or a bunch of daffodils from the garden, in short, of the reassurance that their existence has some value because it is of consequence to at least one fellow human being.

Clubs may be linked with visiting, in so far as some of them keep in touch with their older members who become housebound, but it is probably true to say that, with exceptions, they cater for the more active and gregarious of the elderly. There are signs that the compulsory gregariousness which once marked them may be on the wane. One of the more remarkable achievements of the past 25 years in club work has been the increase in the range of the possibilities they offer and in the whole concept of what a club should be and do. The danger during what, in this as in so many other departments of life, is likely to be seen later as a transitional stage, is that certain organizers may resist change and continue to cater for those who were old when they were young, and are now mostly dead. The cause of the change is simple enough. No longer are club amenities and activities envisaged as something which the privileged and competent provide for the benefit of the under-privileged and incompetent, even though there may still be a small place for this kind of benevolent autocracy.

Bearing in mind that the type of English club has always been a stronghold of the privileged, it is curious that this atmosphere of patronage should have grown up around old people's clubs, particularly when the earliest of them had so much in common with those which cluster in the West End of London. Groups of elderly and leisured-by-retirement men used to gather in the shelters of public parks in the Midlands, to talk or to smoke in amiable silence according to mood, in either case to escape from the feminine flurry of their homes. In the early years of the present century, the Sons of Rest movement put roofs of their own over some of these groups and the first clubs for old people were in being. Something similar happened in Scotland about the same time, this club being for elderly cabbies. (It is worth noting that all these were for men only, whereas the membership of today's mixed clubs is almost always heavily overweighted with women, not all of whom are widows.) The next traceable development came in 1927, when, in Manchester, Liverpool and other industrial cities, social workers arranged social afternoons for old people who were badly housed and badly off. The seed of clubs as we know them today had been sown. By the end of the war it was in healthy growth; during the fifteen years or so that followed came the harvest. Nobody knows the exact number of clubs in existence today, but it is probably over 9,000, ranging in type from the group of twenty or so which meets one afternoon a fortnight in a hired room in a country pub to a purpose-built centre serving a city area, open all day six days a week and providing every possible facility from meals and baths to chiropody and hairdressing, from the more usual entertainments to opportunities to practice handicrafts or join classes of one kind or another.

Withal, it has been estimated that not more than 20 per cent of the elderly population at the outside join clubs. To wonder why is not to imply that salvation lies in clubs alone; there are some people, old or young, to whom they will never appeal. But it is hard to believe that 80 per cent of the pensionable population is inherently unclubbable; it seems more likely that there is a proportion who stay outside because they feel, often quite rightly, that the only accessible club offers nothing that would appeal to them. To begin with, they are not over eager to belong to a group calling itself Darby and Joan, or Silver Threads Among the Gold, or Sunlight at Eventide, or even worse. They are not passionate about bingo, they may drink coffee or beer in preference to tea, they do not particularly want to spend an afternoon in a public hall sitting in a chair a good deal less comfortable than they can command at home, they agree that it is admirable to arrange out-of-season holidays at reduced terms for pensioners but they personally, it may be for quite good reasons, do not happen to want to go on that kind of holiday. On the other hand they might be delighted to join a club that provided, according to taste, some intellectual stimulus, a comfortable meeting place where they could be sure of meeting compatible acquaintances, more newspapers, magazines and reviews than they could afford to buy for themselves, a chance to see a TV programme in company, simple but really appetizing meals (an acceptance in this country that food is a legitimate source of pleasure, even though a minor pleasure, and not merely 'nourishment' would help so much here) and abundant warmth.

The big day clubs, which provide all this and more, are never short of members. There is, obviously, a limit to the extent to which they can be multiplied, but there is growing support for the relatively small neighbourhood 'drop-in' club, which, wherever it has been set up and attractively furnished and equipped, has been found to fill a need. There are possibilities here in the conversion of an ordinary family house; this has been done most successfully in some areas, where it has been found that the number of small rooms makes possible a wider range of activities and enjoyable inactivities and that a homelike atmosphere is virtually built in. A garden—and many old town houses have neglected but promising gardens—can be an asset, providing at once an attraction to men members, who will make its care their responsibility, and the chance of a seat in the sun for the more elderly who may find the walk to the nearest park too far.

Some of the big daily clubs operate also as day centres, where the frail elderly are brought from their homes to spend the period from mid-morning until late afternoon. Where they exist they often defer the day when the frail elderly have to enter a home. Such a task is beyond the competence of the small drop-in clubs, but it is possible that many of them could extend their usefulness if they laid on transport occasionally for those who, while not housebound, find a journey of any distance more than they can manage. It is this kind of flexibility in the face of local need, which is one of the marks of a good old people's club.

Some clubs have handicraft groups which may turn out work

of a standard to be sold in the open market. All day centres include in their programme some kind of occupational therapy, which usually means simple craft work. Neither should be confused with workshops for old people, though, certainly, the workshops often have something of the social atmosphere of a club. It had long been realized that there were many elderly people who would benefit from some employment after retiring age. A few of the lucky ones, almost all men, were able to realize the ideal of a gradual withdrawal from work, rather than an abrupt retirement, because their employers had followed the pioneering example of Messrs Rubery Owen. This engineering firm of Darlaston, South Staffordshire, has, since 1949, provided work for some of its pensionable employees in the Sons of Rest workshops, where the tempo is gentler than in the main works. These were a minority of those who wanted work after retiring age. Some found themselves new, full-time jobs. More undertook part-time or odd jobs. In the last countrymen had an advantage. It is too easy to romanticize rural living, but farm work does provide a variety of occasional jobs suited to the elderly. In towns there were many who were unfit for a full week's work even if they could have found it, who were yet bored by idleness and deteriorated rapidly when they lost the companionship that had gone with their jobs. For them, in 1951, the Finsbury Borough Council, in conjunction with the Employment Fellowship, started its Employment Scheme for the Elderly, whose original inspiration came from the Borough's MOH, Dr Blyth Brooke. This started in a rented house; soon it had its own building, open for two hours morning and afternoon, where elderly men and women did various light jobs for local manufacturers. They were paid ten shillings a week which, as an addition to pension was not to be despised, but far more important was the sense of purpose and independence fostered. Today there are more than sixty such workshops in various parts of the country. Few are self supporting – the Old People's Workshop at High Wycombe is one of the few which meets its running costs out of profits – and most need fairly substantial grants. There are the occasional doubts about 'exploitation', which usually attach to outwork from factories, and, increasingly these days, the old people's workshops must compete for such tasks with the rather similar schemes set up in a number of mental hospitals. But there is no doubt of the need for sheltered jobs of this kind, whose effect can be so good that it is not unknown for old people to graduate from them back into normal work in industry.

Whether, in ten years time, we shall still have more than 9,000 clubs, or more, or far fewer, it would be rash to prophesy. What is certain is that those which have justified their survival, or which may come into being, will be clubs which see their work largely in terms of providing the opportunity for their elderly members to do things for themselves, to develop new interests as well as maintain the old, and, as far as possible, to run their own affairs. The lingering 'Darby and Joan' image tends to obscure the fact that many club members are in their spry early sixties and that, far from being numbered among the helpless, they are an excellent source of recruits for work among those twenty and even thirty years their seniors.

CHAPTER XIII

The Organization of Housing
the Elderly

Local authorities have a duty to provide residential accommodation for people who, 'by reason of age, infirmity . . . are in need of care and attention . . . not otherwise available to them'. In other words, as they were reminded in the Ministry of Health Memorandum: The Care of the Elderly in Hospital and Residential Homes, circulated in 1965, residential accommodation should be planned only for those who are no longer able to maintain themselves in their own homes, even with all possible help from the domiciliary services, but who do not need hospital care. While it is true that, today, the average age of the residents is higher than it was in the years immediately after the war and that there is a correspondingly higher degree of frailty among them, it is very doubtful indeed whether they all meet the condition of the Ministry's Memorandum. Ten years ago Peter Townsend *(The Last Refuge)* found that 'between a half and two-thirds (were) comparatively active and (were) physically and mentally capable of managing most or all personal and household tasks with little or no help'.

For the residents, every residential home, the good equally with the bad, represents a failure. By coming into a home they have given up the key of their own front door, and with it something of their individuality. From now until the end of their lives they must live as members of a community which they entered as strangers, and they have, inevitably, renounced a large part of the possibility of exercising choice which is the essence of free will.

If this point seems to be laboured, it is deliberately so. In face of the statements occasionally heard from members of local authorities that all the old people living in their modern, purpose-built homes are as happy as the day is long, it is well sometimes to remind ourselves of the truth of the situation. The best of residential homes can be no more than a second best.

Having admitted that, one may justifiably take pleasure in how good the second best can be and how varied the forms it can take. There is no stereotype for a good residential home, any more than there is a stereotype for its residents, but it is easily enough recognized. One admirable home was a house in the grounds of a convent in the North West where four elderly, though relatively active gentlemen were looked after by an Irish nun only a few years younger than themselves. Its centre was a comfortable kitchen, with a rag rug and a budgerigar, where, most of the year, there was an open fire in the grate and most of the day a kettle simmering on the hob. Each of the residents had his own latchkey, each was a personality to the nun. Besides telling her their respective family histories, in which she was deeply interested, they were able to retail information about life in the big city outside, and such innovations as evening football matches by floodlighting.

Another was a local authority home in what was once a manufacturing magnate's mansion in the leafy suburb of an industrial city where a genteel – it is the only word – maiden lady spent the last two or three years of her long life. 'When are the times that my friend may come to see me?' she asked diffidently on the day after her arrival, when she was saying good-bye to a visitor who had called to find out how she was settling. 'Any time she likes, Miss X,' replied the matron. 'This is your home. It wouldn't be very convenient before ten o'clock in the morning, but I don't suppose that would be very convenient for her either.' It proved, indeed, to be Miss X's home. Not an ideal one; to the end she regretted having to share a bedroom. But from it she went off to spend a holiday with a friend and to it she returned to tell her stories of how she had enjoyed herself. She was soon involved in small jobs ('Matron relies on me to do the salts and peppers and mustards for the tables every day'). She died in hospital because her last illness called for hospital treatment. While there she frequently said 'I want to go home', to the matron and to a member of the staff of the home, both of whom visited her regularly. When she died there was a wreath from the home at her funeral and some relatives who came from a distance were courteously received by the matron who introduced them to Miss X's special friends among the residents. Finally, arrangements were made for those friends to attend the funeral service. It is difficult to think of anything that could have been more reassuring for the other residents most of whom were sufficiently realistic to admit that their own funerals could not be so far distant, than the warmth and dignity of that occasion.

That has been described at some length as a good, though by no means unique example of what a small home for old people may hope to be. The less good err usually – apart, that is, from defects in the personality of the staff, and, in particular, of the matron, which may militate against a homelike atmosphere – in being over-protective, in failing to encourage, even when they do not positively discourage initiative among residents, in subordinating the wishes, even if they are unexpressed, of those residents to administrative convenience. To a matron with a housewifely soul, rooms furnished alternately in light oak and fumed oak are far more attractive than rooms crammed with the heterogeneous furniture which residents have brought with them, but it is the memories of a lifetime which are being banished with the woodworm – and that can be treated anyway. To a matron who is responsible for the health of residents, it is obviously an advantage to have one general practitioner looking after all of them, but, by making such an arrangement she may be robbing an old lady of a doctor who is the confidant of half a lifetime, who is the only person she now knows who remembers her husband, and with whom she may allow herself the relief of saying that she thinks Matron is an old bag. When residents are rather tottery it is obviously risky to allow them to boil kettles to make themselves a pot of tea or coffee, but, if in a home on the outskirts of London which cares for very old Polish ladies, every resident can have an electric kettle in her bed-sitting room, is it really impossible for local authority small homes to provide a utility room where old ladies can make tea and perhaps do minor washing and pressing too? Details like this, ultimately, are the decision of local administrators, however urgently Ministry circulars may plead for single bed-sitting rooms for all residents unless they specifically ask to share a

room, for the right to bring in furniture and personal possessions, for the right, common to every other NHS patient, to have
the doctor of one's choice. Time and money permitting, it might
bring about a transformation if all matrons and local authority
administrators made a tour of homes in Scandinavia or Germany,
where bed-sitting rooms are taken for granted and hobbies
encouraged may include oil painting, pursued so energetically
that the artist's room is lined three deep with canvases stacked
against the wall.

The standing reproach of our day, however, is not such
details but the fact that more than 20,000 of the old people in
residential accommodation are still in what were old workhouse
buildings.

True, a good deal has been done to improve them, but
their whole plan imposes fairly strict limits on what can be
done, the atmosphere of the workhouse lingers, if only in the
minds of the old residents and their relatives, and, as Peter
Townsend has shown in his survey of residential institutions
and homes for the aged (*The Last Refuge*), there is no doubt
that surroundings do have some effect on the attitudes of staff.
While these buildings remain in use there will be cause to
deplore our provision for the elderly.

In the new homes the most urgent problems are related to the
acute difficulty, shared by most residential institutions, of
recruiting staff, and, linked with it, the changing character of
the residents. It may be that if the recommendations of the
Williams Committee on the training and qualification of staff,
which would mean that those entering the service could work
for a recognized qualification and look forward to a career structure, are carried out, recruiting will show an improvement. It is
certain that there must be an increasing use of part-time staff,
and that residential workers will be largely replaced by non-
residents coming in for a night shift as they might to a hospital
ward. Perhaps there is a pattern for the future in the experiment
carried out at Finchley, where, in a large converted house,
which the Finchley Senior Citizens Housing Society bought, six
old people needing more care than can be guaranteed for them
in their own homes are looked after by a matron and an assistant matron, whose 'staff' are the relatives of the residents,
working a rota. There are now plans for a day centre, run on

similar lines, which will extend help to other families with old people who cannot be left alone.

None of these developments can alter the acute difficulties created by the increasing age and frailty of the residents. The small homes established in the first years after the war were set up in often rather sketchily adapted houses, mostly with no lifts and too little ground floor accommodation. They were originally intended for the relatively young old, those in their seventies or even the later sixties, who, for one reason or another, were homeless or unable to continue in their own homes. Such of those first residents who still survive are now well into their eighties. Those who are coming into them are for the most part about the same age, or, if younger, are frail and infirm, for, with improved domiciliary services and more housing designed for the needs of the elderly, they are able to continue in their own homes until a later stage. Though they do not—or should not—need skilled nursing, other than the kind of short-term nursing which a district nurse would provide if an elderly person was ill in his or her own home, they need more and more care and attention and help with the daily details of life. They cannot manage stairs; they cannot get in or out of the bath unaided; to complicate the situation still further, they may be failing mentally. The difference between a residential home for old people and a nursing home for old people becomes narrow indeed in such circumstances. How acute is the need for accommodation for the aged and infirm is indicated not only by the waiting lists for the local authority homes, which have about 80,000 beds, of which the majority are in small homes, and for those run by the voluntary societies, which have another 18,000, but by the fact that there are another 10,000 or so beds in registered private homes in England and Wales, of which by far the greater number are occupied by the elderly. (Figures quoted in *Private Homes for Old People*, published by the National Corporation for the Care of Old People, 1967 and Townsend: *The Last Refuge*.) Still there are waiting lists, still the relatives of mentally frail and possibly incontinent old people find it desperately difficult to get suitable accommodation for them.

It is probable that the range of standards, from the very good to the deplorable, is wider in the private homes than in those publicly provided, but it is difficult to recommend the wholesale closure of the less desirable ones when there is no practicable alternative for their residents. There is growing interest at the moment in the idea that local authorities might find it possible to pay the fees of some of their residents in the way that local authority children's departments sometimes supplement their own accommodation by paying for a child to be cared for by one of the voluntary children's societies. If it were to become a reality, it might bring with it stricter standards of inspection which could have the effect of raising the overall level of private homes. Could it be stretched to cover the considerable number of residential hotels where the average age of residents is so high that they are, in effect, old people's homes which lack adequate staff, adequate equipment and suitable premises? And if they were closed, where would the aged guests go? It is the merciless logic of numbers which, at present, makes for the persistence of a situation which is far from satisfactory.

Besides the constant demand for permanent places, residential homes are increasingly being asked to provide short-term accommodation. Sometimes this is to give relief to a family which is caring for an elderly relative at home, sometimes for a short illness, sometimes to help a frail elderly couple, normally just able to manage in their own home, through the bronchial winter months. There are hospital geriatric departments which already do this for the more severely disabled. At Langthorne and Whipps Cross Hospitals, London, there has been established a scheme of 'Six weeks in: six weeks out', which the geriatric consultant, Dr J. DeLargy, set up with the dual aim of rehabilitating the aged and relieving their relatives. There has in fact been only limited success with physical rehabilitation but six weeks stay in the atmosphere of an active and cheerful geriatric unit, with the assurance of a return home at the end of that time, improves the morale of elderly patients who may have led rather isolated lives at home. For their relatives, the certainty of six weeks during which they can lead a normal family and social life does a great deal to relieve the strain of the 'duty' periods. Such a regularly alternating system would hardly be practical, or even necessary, for homes, but it is easy to envisage the possibility that it might become standard practice to plan for two or three temporary visitors among the normal population of most old people's homes. There are many occasions, varying from holidays, or the illness of some other member of the family to something as mundane as the decorators coming in, when the knowledge that an elderly parent or other relative would be welcome at the residential home would be a relief to many households.

Whether it is desirable to link housing for old people with an old people's home, say by building bungalows in the grounds of the home, with main meals available for the tenants in the central building, is a question on which opinion, in this country at least, remains divided. Supporters of the idea argue that familiarity with the residential home makes the transfer to it easier for the tenants of the bungalows when they become too infirm to carry on alone any longer. Opponents quote the experience of authorities which have built grouped bungalows with a warden in charge. Rarely do their tenants have to transfer, and when they do it is almost always to hospital for care during a terminal illness. There is not, however, any very large body of evidence on the subject. Figures apart, some find repugnant the idea that the elderly in bungalows should daily contemplate the still more elderly in a home, with the prospect of joining them in a few years time. Holland has at least one excellently planned scheme – speaking materially – where flats suitable for different degrees of capacity or incapacity are neighboured by a hospital for old people. The British visitor may have a moment of wondering whether, round the next corner, there is an attractive funeral parlour, but, in fairness, the atmosphere is anything but gloomy, and there is, of course, no suggestion that old people who enter the flats for the relatively active will necessarily make the same graduated recession. But many may feel more natural sympathy with the recommendation of a county medical officer who, speaking from experience, said that if a residential home had land to spare the thing to build on it was an infant welfare clinic rather than housing for another group of the elderly.

Literally, perhaps, that advice can seldom be followed, but the principle it embodies, that homes for the elderly should be part of the everyday world rather than gerontological reserves, is universally valid. Sometimes simple means can help to uphold it. A London home, opening on to a busy street, made known that, on weekday mornings, tea and biscuits were available for a copper or two. The result was a regular trickle of local women looking in for a chat with their former neighbours on their way home from shopping. With more encouragement, also help in getting there, it is possible that a number of residents of homes might enjoy an occasional afternoon at a local old people's club. Perhaps the club might sometimes hold a meeting at the home. The kind of fraternizing that might be expected to result would, perhaps, be easier than the relations between residents and outside visitors who may have little in common.

It is worth considering some seldom quoted figures which were recalled at the 1966 National Conference of the NOPWC by Mr R. Huws Jones, Principal, National Institute for Social Work Training. In Britain, he told his hearers, official policy on the care of the elderly was that all possible services should be provided to enable them to stay in their own homes. In fact, whereas in 1951 just under ten per 1,000 people of pensionable age were living in homes, in 1961 the number was fourteen per 1,000. By 1976 is was estimated that twenty per 1,000 would be living in homes.

The reasons, Mr Huws Jones went on to point out, included the obvious one that the proportion of old people in the population is increasing – in the next twenty years there will be one million more old people aged seventy-five or over. Also, modern hospital treatment means that many of the elderly who, formerly, would have spent their last years bedridden in a chronic sick ward, are now able to leave it but still may need more care than they are able to provide for themselves. The numbers will increase also because supply creates demand. Today all who are concerned with the subject know that there are many people who want and probably need to go into homes who are unable to find a place in one, but nobody knows how many. As the number of homes grows, the real extent of the need will be revealed. And as homes are seen to be good – this is to assume that the quality will continue to improve – more people are likely to want to enter one. Holland has notably good homes, and the proportion of old people in them is about four times as high as that in Britain, Mr Huws Jones told the conference.

If such a situation were to arise here it would, one hopes,

be the very reverse of the result of a policy of 'pushing old people into homes'. It would mean, rather, that an increasing number of old people had made a positive choice to spend their later years in a home and that an increasing number and variety of homes had enabled them to find one that suited them.

CHAPTER XIV

Hospitals

The word geriatrics entered the common vocabulary in the late nineteen forties, and, from the first, it had for the public an aura of magic. The medicine of old age was, of course, not magical, nor even new. Good doctors had always known that illness in old age, like illness in infancy or adolescence, had certain features peculiar to itself. In other words, if two patients were suffering from the same disease, their respective treatments must take into account the fact that one of them was fifteen months, the other seventy-nine years old.

Two things combined to bring the subject into prominence at the time. The establishment of the National Health Service, in 1948, made active medical treatment accessible to large numbers of people who, practically speaking, had never previously received it. Coincidentally, the mid-twentieth century saw also the beginnings of chemo-therapy, the discovery of drugs which were potent curative agents, so that, to take the most obvious example, an attack of pneumonia was no longer regarded as a death sentence for the elderly. Hence the reports of 'medical miracles' and the incidental fostering of that credulousness about 'science' which is one of the marks of our time. There is nothing miraculous about the fact, rediscovered about this period, that, given proper care, and, even more importantly, individual attention, the elderly sick are likely to improve, though usually, they do not do so with the speed of the young sick.

A report printed by the Bradford (B) Hospital Management Committee at the end of 1949 (An Investigation and Analysis of 701 Chronic Sick and Elderly Patients in Bradford Hospitals, including a Scheme for a Geriatric Service) which had less publicity at the time than it deserved, puts the situation perfectly. With the establishment of the NHS the Management Committee had inherited, along with other responsibilities, the hospital sections of the two Bradford Institutions, in common parlance, two workhouse infirmaries. Of these, the authors of the report, Mr Peter McEwen, consulting surgeon and Dr S. G. Laverty, medical registrar, who examined them, with the patients of a third hospital, 701 in all, wrote: 'Little was known about them as a group except that most were aged, many were bedridden, and, in general, a poor opinion was held of their powers of recovery. The treatment of these patients presented a problem the magnitude of which was uncertain. To ascertain what might be done for them, it was first necessary to find out what type of patients they were and how they had got into hospital. Their disabilities had to be carefully estimated, and the hospital system under which they were cared for had to be critically examined, for it was known to be inferior in many respects to that of the acute hospitals.'

It was a description which, at that time, could have been applied to virtually every Public Assistance Institution in the country, and, between them, they were sheltering – it is a more accurate term than treating – about 60,000 old people (figure quoted by Sir Ernest Rock Carling at the NOPWC's conference in November, 1946). Only at a very few hospitals had enlightened doctors shown what could be achieved by proper diagnosis and treatment of the aged sick, and by proper provision for their convalescence and rehabilitation. The work of Dr Marjory Warren at the West Middlesex Hospital, which had been going on for about fifteen years, has already been mentioned. At Orsett Lodge Hospital, Essex, Mr Cosin, who was a surgeon, not a physician, and who, as a consequence of evacuation, found himself responsible for a number of aged 'chronic sick' patients, managed to get about half of them out of bed within a few weeks, and some, 'who were sent into his hospital to die eventually walked out on their own feet'. At St Helier Hospital, Dr E. B. Brooke arranged the closest co-operation between the hospital and the home-care services so that elderly patients, like any other patients, stayed in hospital only as long as they needed the treatment and facilities of a hospital and otherwise were cared for in long-stay annexes if that were necessary, or in their own homes. At St John's Hospital, Battersea, Dr Trevor Howell had instituted a vigorous scheme of rehabilitation for the 20 per cent or so of his elderly patients who were classed as chronic sick. Of the other 80 per cent who had entered hospital, he had found that 40 per cent would get better fairly quickly and 40 per cent would get worse and die. He was able to compare his elderly patients with the Pensioners of the Chelsea Hospital, elderly men who had to pass a fitness test before admission, and so judge which disabilities were indeed due to 'old age', or were particularly common among the elderly, and which to ailments which might be suffered at any age. These, with others, formed, in 1947, a Medical Society for the Care of the Elderly, whose name was later changed to British Geriatric Society. Earlier, the British Medical Association had set up a committee to investigate existing provision for the treatment and care of the elderly, and/or infirm, which it believed to be 'inadequate', a word which hardly erred in the direction of overstatement. Its two reports, published respectively in 1947 and 1948, recommended the establishment of geriatric units within the hospital service, including out-patient clinics and 'half-way houses' for patients who had not yet recovered sufficiently to be discharged to their own homes. The Government accepted the recommendations in general, and, when the NHS came into being, encouraged the fourteen Regional Hospital Boards to create geriatric units. They have done so, but their quality is perhaps even more variable than that of general hospitals. To call a chronic ward a geriatric unit does not really do anything very much for either its atmosphere or its results. Proper premises and proper equipment are obviously necessary, but in themselves they are not enough. This, almost more than any other, is a branch of medicine in which personal factors are highly important. It was not by chance that the pioneer geriatric units were directed by remarkable doctors who, among their other gifts, possessed the power of inspiring and energizing those with whom they worked. They needed both, as their successors still do, for there are obstacles to the progress of this specialized branch of general medicine. Teaching hospitals, traditionally, have been loath to treat the aged sick (this is a venerable tradition – Guy's Hospital was founded to take the aged sick whom St Thomas's could not, or did not wish to cope with), therefore neither with doctors nor with nurses has the medicine of old age enjoyed any great status.

The medical profession being innately conservative, those practising the more established specialities referred to the new geriatric consultants as 'jumped up GP's' – and, indeed, if they were to be good at the job they needed the pastoral sense which is the mark of the first-class GP. The nursing care of the old was a demanding task and removed from the newest developments which attracted keen young student nurses. The elderly patients included a large percentage of those who were poor as well as infirm and they were often nursed in buildings to which the aura of pauperdom still attached.

Against all that, the best of the geriatric units show an example which is exciting as well as inspiring. Some of them have day hospitals attached (a day hospital differs from a day centre in that it almost always gives treatment as well as caring for the elderly), which cater both for patients on their way out of the unit and others who, by spending their days under its supervision, are able to defer, and sometimes altogether to avoid admission. Attendances in geriatric out-patient clinics have greatly increased, and the units themselves are dealing with more patients. But still, in its 1964 annual report (and it could be re-written today) the NOPWC was expressing concern at the 'grave lack of accommodation in certain parts of the country for those elderly people needing nursing care. . . . Many instances have been brought to the Council's notice where a hospital bed was not available and the amount of nursing care needed was beyond that available in a residential home. This left no alternative but the private nursing home at fees far beyond the purse of the old person concerned, even with National Assistance supplementation towards maintenance and possible contributions from the family.'

Nevertheless, the number of old people who are to be found in private nursing homes is a great deal higher than may generally be realized. In their study, Nursing Homes in England and Wales, published by the National Corporation for the Care of Old People, Caroline Woodroffe and Peter Townsend state that, in 1960 in England and Wales, there were nearly 1,200 registered nursing homes, with just under 18,700 beds, of which 1,600 were maternity and 17,000 other. Also there were well over 100 voluntary homes with about 5,500 beds, which were exempt from registration, or were entitled to exemption even if it were not granted by the local authority concerned. The survey showed that 60 per cent of the patients in a sample of 16 voluntary homes were elderly, and 87 per cent of a sample of 132 private homes catered mainly or entirely for elderly patients.

The Council went on to note that 'part of the difficulty seems to result from the division of responsibility between hospital and local authorities. Each can refuse to accept the old person on the grounds that his or her care should be undertaken by the other authority'. This sentence, too, might have stood in any report issued by the Council from its founding to the present day. The existence of certain brilliant examples of team work, linking hospital with general practitioner and domiciliary services, shows that the tri-partite division of the Health Service is not an absolute bar to efficient functioning. But it is an excuse for inefficiency – sometimes readily seized – and, at best, it makes the task of all concerned in the care of the sick more laborious. In geriatric medicine above all, whose effectiveness is indissolubly linked to factors like proper housing and good domiciliary services, it is to be deplored. One of its aspects, the separation of the hospital doctor from the general practitioner, has a particular bearing on the well-being of the old, for it is on a creative tension between them that good medicine for the old should depend. The hospital doctor, knowing that, today, there exist for old people possibilities of treatment, including operations which, twenty years ago, would never have been dreamed of, is inclined to feel that if a procedure is possible it should be carried out.

He needs his GP colleague to point out that, possible or not, for this particular old person at this particular time, the procedure is not desirable. Similarly, the GP, from long experience of seeing the old 'living with their disabilities', may lean over too far in the direction of leaving half-well alone, and would benefit from prodding. The patient would benefit most of all.

The division has, too, its share of responsibility for what is perhaps the most shaming area of our hospital provision today, the department of psycho-geriatrics. Periodically the conscience of the public is stirred by newspaper articles describing conditions in the old people's wards of certain mental hospitals. Two things may be said at once about these. Nobody who knows this side of the hospital service would be willing to deny the truth of such accusations. Equally, if they knew the service well, they would be prepared to maintain that such depths are not typical. At the other extreme there are psycho-geriatric units which are models of efficiency and humanity. They are not typical either. The mean is a desperate struggle to maintain reasonable standards in often unsuitable buildings with always insufficient staff. It is noticeable that, in the best units, co-operation embraces not only the other branches of the Health Service but every ounce of voluntary help that can be mustered in the district.

The absence of co-operation accounts for one feature of the situation which is less often publicized but which is, overall, more damaging even than the existence here and there of regrettable standards. This is that, because there is no overall provision for assessing accurately whether any given patient needs psychiatric or geriatric care, a number of the elderly may find themselves in the wrong hospital. A survey of hospitals serving the City of Belfast made fairly recently gave grounds for believing that 24 per cent of the sample of patients in mental hospitals had been misplaced and 34 per cent of those in the geriatric unit. Experience in other departments suggests that we shall have to wait for assessment units in any number; meantime in some areas – including Birmingham Region – there are some joint appointments which enable geriatricians to work part time in the mental hospitals.

CHAPTER XV

The Future Years

When, soon after the outbreak of the Second World War, the National Old People's Welfare Council (or Committee, as it was then called, and from 1970 a fully independent organization) came into being, there were three outstanding problems connected with the elderly. There was a lack of proper housing for them; there was a lack of trained staff to care for those who could not care for themselves; there was a lack of accommodation in homes and hospitals organized for their particular needs. Additionally, in some of the homes and hospitals which did exist, the standards left a great deal to be desired.

Today, almost thirty years later, there are still three outstanding problems connected with the welfare of the elderly. There is not enough proper housing for them; there are not enough trained staff – nor, indeed, enough staff, trained or untrained – to care for those who cannot care for themselves; there is not enough accommodation in homes and hospitals organized for their particular needs. Additionally, in some of the homes and hospitals which do exist, the standards leave a good deal to be desired.

To put the situation so brutally is not to be pessimistic, still less is it to underrate the enormous progress which has been made during those thirty years, progress in public attitudes as much as in material provision. It is difficult to believe that it is only a generation ago that the newly-founded Committee for the Welfare of the Aged was fighting for pocket money for old people in chronic sick hospitals and that the Ministry of Health was thinking of evacuating the elderly from London and billeting numbers of them in empty houses where they would be left to look after themselves. The horrified disbelief with which both facts would be received today by those whose memories do not stretch so far back is in itself a measure of the distance we have travelled. It is no more than realistic to

acknowledge that certain problems are, of their very nat[
continuing.

In a country which has an overall housing shortage and
whose industrial cities have a formidable backlog of slum clear-
ance the elderly must take their place in the queue, and that
place is never likely to be at the head. In a society which offers
other, more obviously attractive kinds of employment, it is unlikely that work with the elderly will have an overplus of
recruits in a time of full employment. When institutions,
whether homes or hospitals, care for those who, almost by
definition, are helpless and often friendless also, there is always
a danger that standards may slip and a possibility that they may
deteriorate unpardonably. These are the constants of a task
which will always expand beyond the existing provision, if only
because expectations rise with that provision. In moments of
discouragement it is permissible to remind ourselves that Britain
today is generally considered to be among the world's leaders
in work for old people, and that our problems are not peculiar
to this country. In an illustrated newspaper article on a new and
admirable home for old people at Kristinehamn, in Sweden (The
Times, June 29, 1967) its social welfare officer was quoted as
saying that it 'desperately' needed more trained workers to take
care of them. Also, the home had a long waiting list.

There is no doubt that our long tradition of voluntary social
work has played a large part in bringing us to that leading
position. Without the brilliant creative initiative of the great
pioneer figures of voluntary social service and without the faith-
ful continuing concern of tens of thousands less distinguished,
the Welfare State would be a poorer thing than it is today. At
present, despite the financial crises that are endemic in our
economy, there are grounds for hoping that it may in the future
become a much better thing and that Old People's Welfare will
share in the general improvement. Over the past twenty-five
years or so work for old people has grown up as part of the
general health and welfare services, and, inevitably, has suffered
from the piecemeal fashion in which those services have
developed.

Nevertheless, the six authors of a detailed comparative study
of old people in Britain, Denmark and the USA (Old People in
Three Industrial Societies, Routledge and Kegan Paul. Authors:

Ethel Shanas, Peter Townsend, Dorothy Wedderburn, Henning Friis, Poul Milhoj, Jan Stehouwerk) found that, in Britain, the elderly saw more of their doctors and got more help at home when they were ill than did the elderly in the other countries examined. Now there are prospects of developments which should help to get rid of the fragmentation which is one of the major disabilities of the present complex of services. The Ministry of Health's Green Paper, published in July, 1968 as a basis for discussion, proposed reducing to a far smaller number the 700 or so authorities then concerned in health matters. It suggested that if they were forty or fifty, they would be big enough to allow large-scale planning. Each of these units would be responsible for the whole range of health services in its area. Dissent from various quarters was quickly made known. In particular there were objections to the size of the proposed new units, which critics felt must lead to remote administration. The legislation which ultimately emerges is likely to depart in a number of ways from the suggestions of the Green Paper – the Minister, since its publication, has said in Parliament that he was considering some kind of two-tier system. Two of its basic principles can hardly be seriously questioned. They are that resources must be used as efficiently, which means as economically as possible and that comprehensive health care must mean a single responsible authority covering hospitals, home treatment and the various kinds of community services. In so far as the proposals of the Green Paper are intended to bring the general practitioner into closer contact with both hospitals and local authorities and to give Medical Officers of Health a chance to practise preventive medicine as 'community physicians' they could hardly fail to make available to the old, who, with the chronic sick, have most need of it, a more effective system of home care.

The Report of the Seebohm Committee, which was even more closely concerned with work for the elderly, was published on the same day as the Green Paper. It was the result of two and a half years' study of the situation and the NOPWC had been invited to give evidence to the committee.

Its brief had been 'to review the organization and responsibilities of the local authority personal social services in England and Wales and to consider what changes are desirable to secure an effective family service'. Not surprisingly, it, too, found that divided responsibility was the source of many weaknesses in the present structure. To remedy them the committee recommended that every major local authority should set up a Social Service Department which would take over the existing responsibilities of the Children's and Welfare Departments, with certain functions of the Health, Education and Housing Departments. The NOPWC could only welcome a proposal which should make possible a comprehensive service, but it recognized also the danger that emphasis on a family service might possibly mean that isolated individuals, particularly elderly individuals, many of whose problems arise from the fact that they have no family, might feel that they were overlooked within it. It urged accordingly that a social worker with special responsibility for the elderly should be included in the team for each area of the new Social Service Department and that in each office there should be a regularly staffed reception point for old people who came there with their troubles or inquiries.

A number of the Seebohm Committee's recommendations echoed the NOPWC's own preoccupations. Notably, on housing, the report stressed that residential care for the old should be more and more used as 'a support in time of trouble', which implies short-term accommodation, and that old people should be enabled to stay in their own homes as long as possible. One way of achieving this would be for housing departments to take a far broader view of their duties than do most of them at present. They should give advice on private housing, arrange exchanges from large houses, including those privately owned, to small ones, and be more active in acquiring, repairing and adapting existing property which might then serve the needs of the old.

The NOPWC's experience also sadly supported the Seebohm Committee's findings on the lack of provision for the mentally frail old and the equal lack of professional support and guidance for relatives who looked after them at home. It is probable that many readers of the report were startled to learn that there were 'more old people with serious mental disorders living in their own homes than in all the institutions together'. It is not necessary to agree with all the report's suggested measures for dealing with the situation, in particular the taking over by the new Social Service departments of certain health and education functions, in order to applaud the emphasis they give to this problem.

Government action on the Seebohm recommendation is likely to be delayed until the publication of the Report of the Royal Commission on Local Government. They are obviously inter-dependent, and equally obviously closely linked with the Green Paper and with the Health Services and Public Health Act which was discussed in Chapter VII. How many of the ideas put forward in any of them will be carried out, and after how long a delay, can only be guessed at. The first question, like all reforms, comes down largely to economics; the other, to some extent, is governed by the defensive tactics which, in such cir-cumstances, are inevitably employed by various professional interests. For the present the two reports already published are valuable for the degree to which they express current trends in thinking on the social services and, by so doing, help to con-dition public opinion for new departures. It should be noted that the two reports and the Act also recognize the continuing need for voluntary work and the possibility of its development. The Seebohm Committee thinks the new Social Service depart-ments should help 'vigorous, outward-looking voluntary associa-tions which can demonstrate good standards of service, provide opportunities for appropriate training for their workers, both professional and voluntary, and show a flair for innovation'.

If the requirements sound exacting they only confirm what the NOPWC, like other voluntary associations, has long known, that, in a society where the State provides welfare services, voluntary bodies will survive only in so far as they deserve to. It is fairly safe to prophesy that a similar message will come from the Aves Committee, which is expected to report in the autumn of 1969. Its terms of reference were: 'To enquire into the role of voluntary workers in the social services. The Com-mittee will consider particularly how the work of the volunteer fits into the total structure of the personal social services; whether there are new settings where they might help; their relationship to professional workers, questions of recruitment and the different contributions of particular age groups; and any preliminary or continuing need for preparation and guidance.' One development already under way is the direct recruiting by hospitals of voluntary workers who, organized by a professional who is a member of the hospital staff, have shown how varied and effective is the service they can give. Voluntary organizations may not always be entirely happy about this system, which some of their members are likely to see as poaching on their territory. In the interests of the end result one can only hope for a measure of flexibility on both sides.

Alongside the reports we have the prospect of solid legislation in the Government's White Paper on its earnings-related pensions scheme, which, according to the Secretary of State for Social Services, is intended to abolish the division of Britain into 'two nations in old age', those who had had the good luck to be enrolled in good pensions schemes by virtue of their employment and the rest who, towards the end of their lives, had had to apply to the National Assistance Board. The old, Mr Crossman reminded the House of Commons, made up 14 per cent of the nation. They had only 9 per cent of its income and two million of them had an income below the minimum guaranteed by the supplementary benefits commission. While the benefits of the new scheme will be enjoyed only by the next generation of pensioners, at least the existing ones have a guarantee that all pensions will be reviewed regularly every twenty-four months and, as a minimum, adjusted to allow for increases in the cost of living.

For those concerned with work among old people, the new scheme should ensure that, when the NOPWC is preparing to celebrate its Golden Jubilee, primary poverty among pensioners will not be one of the difficulties with which it has to contend. 'Should ensure', let it be noted, not 'will ensure', though it is perhaps being unduly gloomy to envisage an upheaval of the national, perhaps even of the European economy, which will halt if not reverse the current of progress.

For the rest, virtually everything is in question. How can one picture the needs and services of tomorrow when, on the one hand, the age of retirement may be as low as fifty-five, or even fifty, and, on the other, there may be no compulsory age for retirement, the elderly being allowed to taper off gradually by way of shorter working weeks or days, or to change to less exacting jobs which are provided for as a matter of course? It is worth reminding ourselves that, in 1921, when compulsory retirement was not general, 89 per cent of men between sixty-five to sixty-nine years of age and 27 per cent of those over seventy-five were still at work. Granted, adequate pensions were not general either at that time, but it would be rash to assume that all those workers would have been delighted to retire if they could have afforded it. How can one know the structure of society twenty-five years on when we have to balance against each other the universal availability of contraception and the prevalence of early marriages? Will the phenomenon of an increasingly mobile working population mean that more and more of the elderly will be deprived not only of the presence of their younger relatives but of the support, psychological as much as material, of an environment long familiar to them? For the less active, what will be the profit and loss account of more and more central heating and less and less delivery of goods to the door – 'goods' meaning the milk and the morning paper as well as the weekly grocery order? Details as some of them are, all these matters are part of the quality of daily life, and, for the elderly, who do not look far ahead, 'dayliness' becomes increasingly important.

Prospects for the health of the elderly a quarter of a century from now are almost equally an imponderable. A lay public which is almost pathetically credulous about what can be expected from 'science' is apt to think in terms of 'medical miracles'. On this, it is salutary to reflect, as the Office of Health Economics reminded us not long ago, that progress in medicine often comes only when an available procedure is adopted in practice, rather than when a new procedure is first demonstrated to be safe and effective, and that, between those two stages, there may be a lag of many years, or even decades.

It may be that research in gerontology, the study of ageing and its diseases, will bring discoveries about deterioration, whether pathological or 'normal' which would mean not that the average life span would be greatly increased, but that individuals would remain healthy and relatively active during their last years. So far, though the Nuffield Provincial Hospitals Trust has made a capital grant of £10,000 and £5,000 a year for three years for a study under Professor W. Ferguson Anderson, of Glasgow University, gerontology is not a fashionable subject for research. In 1968 Professor Anderson occupied the only university chair of gerontology in the country. At the time of writing there are hopes that three may be established in England, though the projects are still at the stage of discussion.

There are certain possibilities, like, for instance, the discovery of an effective treatment for arthritis, or the development of the kind of vigorous preventive medicine which would cut down the number of chronic bronchitics among the elderly, which might transform the picture. Lacking either it is reasonable to suppose that better living standards and better medical care for today's middle-aged may produce a fitter, more active older generation (the counter argument is that the end of a régime of the survival of the fittest might produce more elderly invalids). They will certainly be better educated and so more confident. One of the changes to which voluntary workers will have to adapt—many of them are already aware of it—is that we are reaching the end of an era in which the aim of voluntary associations was to do things for the elderly and entering one during which they will be engaged in helping the elderly to do things for themselves. It is quite possible that not all those things will be what the associations would have thought of. That is irrelevant. Age brings disadvantages enough without adding to them that of having to accept what others believe to be good for you.

In such a situation, what will be the function of voluntary work for old people? One of its aspects is constant, as the history traced in this book should have made clear. It is always the duty of voluntary bodies to explore, to experiment and to initiate, to point needs, show how they may be met, then hand over to the greater resources of the State. Another aspect is indicated in the reports mentioned earlier in this chapter. Tomorrow even more than today trained voluntary helpers will be needed to work alongside professionals in many departments of the social services, so allowing an expansion of their work that might not otherwise be possible. The word to stress here is 'alongside'. It is time any lingering rivalry between voluntary and statutory professional workers was buried.

There are two features of work for the old, as, indeed, of most other kinds of social work, which are essentially the task of voluntary organizations. The first is providing the 'bespoke services' and taking on the thankless jobs. There will always be individuals whose needs or troubles do not fit into any of the Welfare State's categories. They cannot be tabulated and so they risk falling between the cracks. Volunteers need not tabulate and they are there to fill the cracks. What taking over the thankless jobs may entail has been particularly well put in a small booklet, *The Rôle of the Churches in the Care of the Elderly*, published by the NOPWC in 1968. This suggested that the churches, perhaps before any other body, were fitted to meet, among others, 'the special needs of the least friendly, the least agreeable, the most neglected, the most unsociable, the most intolerant, the most resistant among the old people in our society'. It considered that 'the churches' might be used to denote 'all those who consciously acknowledge their responsibilities to love and serve God and their neighbour'. The definition is broad. It might be expanded still further to include all those voluntary workers, believers or otherwise, who feel a responsibility to love and serve their neighbour.

The second duty of voluntary organizations, and possibly their ultimate justification, is to act as the conscience of society. There are certain truths about social and welfare provision which are never spoken in public because politicians, who are governed by them, are naturally anxious to avoid giving an impression of cynicism. The basic one is that the extent and quality of provision is determined, not by what Royal Commissions recommend or by changes in the administrative system, helpful as both may be, but by how much money is available. That, in turn, depends upon how much the Government of the day feels it can extract from the taxpayer without signing its own death warrant at the next election. There are sharply contested claims on the total and it cannot be assumed that the social services will come at the top of the list. After that first division comes the apportionment of the budgets within the different sections of the individual departments. Here those which can show results are always likely to fare best. Age, having an inevitably unfavourable prognosis, is never likely to have first claim, any more than are the needs of the sub-normal, or of the chronic sick or of long-stay medical patients. The happiness and well-being of the people who come into those categories cannot be expressed in terms of cost benefit analysis. It is for voluntary organizations, besides stimulating Government action by direct contact, to see that their claims are kept before the public. That public is more heedless than heartless. It is given to bursts of indignation when 'scandals' are revealed, be they about conditions in mental hospitals, or old people's homes or children's homes. There is no reason to doubt the sincerity of the indignation or the warmth of the reaction, but, without a constant campaign of information and intelligent propaganda it will die down as quickly as it flared up.

More broadly, in an age which seems irreversibly set towards the worship of certain rather narrowly defined concepts of 'success', towards conformity and towards the mass-produced gratifications of materialism, it may be the vocation of voluntary organizations to proclaim different values, to indicate other ways in which men and women may find happiness, to fight for the right of the individual to be noncomformist to the extent even of being a mild nuisance to his fellows. Mild nuisances are a normal part of human concourse which, if it is to remain vital, should not be reduced to the equivalent of a bland diet.

The organizations which work with the elderly may even feel that part of their task is to reinstate the dignity of 'our bodily death, from which no man living can escape', which St Francis included in his Canticle of 'All Created Things'. The current tendency to regard death as failure and mention of it as a solecism can be small comfort to those who are approaching the natural end of their lives.